I Want a
Hot Fudge Sundae ....
and a Diet Cola

I Want a Hot Fudge Sundae .... and a Diet Cola

CONTRADICTIONS BABY BOOM WOMEN FACE ON TURNING FIFTY

Frieda Farfour Brown, Ph.D. Miriam Grace Mitchell, Ph.D.

This book was printed in the United States of America.

To order additional copies of this book, contact:
Xlibris Corporation
1-888-795-4274
www.Xlibris.com
Orders@Xlibris.com
16444

Contents

ACKNOWLEDGEMENTS

We would like to thank the following for their invaluable contributions to this project. Most important are the women we interviewed whose stories enlightened and entertained us. They provided us with a better understanding of our generation and how we are approaching the second half of our lives.

We are also grateful to these gifted people, without whose encouragement and support, we would have spent more time eating hot fudge sundaes and less time at the computer. Paul Escott patiently provided insightful suggestions, comments, editing and input on each preliminary draft. Doug Waller served as a constant motivator and effective editor for the entire manuscript. We reaped the benefits of the knowledge and experience of these much published authors. Tom Brown supported our efforts at every stage, offering helpful comments and creative ideas. Finally, we are indebted to Laura Hearn, whose timely contribution as we completed the book illustrates some of the most admired qualities of the baby boom generation.

Introduction

I T started with a conversation. A very important conversation about our favorite topic . . . ourselves. Of course we didn't neglect to cover the usual subjects—husbands, children, jobs and extra pounds. In the midst of our discussion, the waiter approached.

"Through with your salads, ladies?"

"Yes."

"Care for dessert?"

We paused, "How about a hot fudge sundae and a diet cola?"

"Make that two."

The waiter left and we burst into laughter. "You would think that two women on the brink of fifty would know better than to order a hot fudge sundae and a DIET cola. We've just been saying how we want to get back into a healthy eating and exercise routine."

"Makes total sense to me!"

What a contradiction! Here we were—two intelligent women, parents of practically grown children, committing diet blasphemy in the midst of a conversation about losing weight. We started to laugh about other parts of our lives that seemed to be full of contradictions. Just that afternoon, one of us had remarked that she had an appointment with the hairdresser to have her hair lightened. "I want to look more natural."

Contradictions. They have defined our lives but also enriched them. We realized that we actually enjoy the many contradictions that make us who we are. We began to wonder: "Are we alone? Or are there other women who think and feel as we do? Is this part of being a baby boomer?" The more we talked, the more our excitement grew. We wanted to know more. Being two college professors used to asking questions about human behavior, we decided to find out.

We decided to seek answers by interviewing fifty women at the age of fifty, born between 1946 and 1954, the early years of the baby boom generation. We focused our study on those who had been trained for careers professionals and those who attended college in the late 60's and early 70's. They represented a diverse group, educationally, geographically and racially.

We developed a questionnaire that explored a wide range of topics, everything from career to family vacations. The survey helped us describe ourselves as a group. Then we asked the women a series of open-ended questions to encourage them to talk freely about their dreams in college and how things have turned out for them up to this point. Each interview lasted approximately two to two and one half hours and we conducted many follow-up interviews as well, asking additional questions. Apparently, we are not the only ones who like to navel gaze— no one we invited to participate refused. These fascinating women readily shared their stories with enthusiasm, wit and wisdom.

As we heard the stories of these women, it became obvious to us that they embraced life to the fullest. They wanted to "win." Win at work, win at home, win at the game of life. Each had chosen her own path to victory. Despite their individuality, we also discovered, to our surprise, distinct patterns in their answers. Different groups of women tended to view life somewhat the same way. We identified seven types of baby boomers, each with its own unique characteristics and contradictions. "Jock talk" may not be the first thing that pops into a woman's head to describe herself—especially when she's turning fifty—but we found athletics to be the perfect metaphor to describe these groups.

The seven sports we chose make different demands of their participants. Some are team activities, some are played by individuals. Some require endurance, others finesse. Some are short matches, others are marathons. The roles our women chose made different demands of them as well. Similarly, some of the women in our study chose unprecedented paths for their lives, some chose traditional ones, while still others chose to study, to sacrifice or to compete in the marketplace. Like athletes, they chose different sports to play, but they all shared a willingness to train, to discipline, and to compete. The decisions they made shaped their futures and the future of our country in significant ways. We believe their stories are worth telling. We hope you will find them as enlightening and instructive as we have.

Frieda Farfour Brown and Miriam Grace Mitchell

PART I

DEFINING THE GAME

Chapter 1

THE DREAMS OF THE BOOMER GENERATION

W_E are our mothers' daughters. We may imagine ourselves to be very different from the conservative, traditional women of the 40's, but our mothers influenced us in ways that would only begin to emerge during our own coming of age in the decade of the 60's. Their legacy to us was complex and ambivalent. As baby boom women redefined what it meant to be a woman at home and at work, they based their dreams on the models and the contradictions already evident in the lives of their mothers. Those who influenced us included not only our biological mothers, but also the many who "mothered" us in significant ways, molding our personalities and influencing our decisions. These mothers believed in us and encouraged us to pursue our dreams. They guided us as we followed paths rarely traveled and nurtured us as we dealt with guilt when we failed. Let's start with Lisa, one of the first women we interviewed for this book. So they could be completely candid with us, we told the women we would use pseudonyms for them and their family members.

Lisa loves and admires her mother, Beth, a woman defined by unselfish devotion to her four children. Beth spent countless hours making their clothes, cooking healthy meals, taking them to school events, checking their homework, and ensuring that they had the opportunity to pursue their dreams whether these were athletic, cultural, social, or educational. She was the epitome of unselfish giving. But there were also powerful messages from Beth. Beth had wanted to be a physician. She told Lisa that given the chance, she would have pursued a medical degree. She had the intellect and the desire, but the culture of the time restricted her choices. Women were rarely accepted into medical school, and their families were not likely to spend their limited resources educating women who were destined to be housewives and mothers.

It wasn't that Beth didn't work. In fact, she worked constantly caring for the children, helping her husband in his business, teaching part-time, and volunteering in the community. Hers was a life of unrecognized and unappreciated work. Lisa found that her mother's honesty profoundly affected her. Beth was happy but had regrets. Lisa didn't want to look back at her life feeling she had missed opportunities.

Lisa also remembers lessons she learned from observing her mother's family. Beth had two sisters who held traditional jobs, one a secretary, the other a social worker. Both were talented, so much so that one could have been a concert pianist, the other a psychiatrist. Their brother became a noted journalist for The Washington Post, realizing both his dreams and his potential. Two generations earlier, Lisa's grandmother, Ellen, had gone to college, which was very rare for the time. She taught briefly before devoting her life to her family. During Lisa's formative years, Ellen encouraged her to read, study and achieve, laying the foundation for Lisa's later success as a student. But her grandmother's brother had an important job at the Rockefeller Foundation. His achievements in medicine brought him a decoration from the Queen of England. In Lisa's family, as in most families at the time, the men, not the women, had rewarding professional careers.

Like Lisa, many of the boomers had talented mothers and grandmothers who shaped their lives. Their willingness to share openly their disappointments as well as their satisfactions taught their daughters and granddaughters to pursue fulfillment both at home and in a profession. Baby boomers accepted that doing both would take work and weren't afraid of the challenge. As one boomer told us, "The women in my family always knew what it was to work; they just didn't work in quite the same ways that I have."

Fifty Women: Our Boomers

We, the baby boom women born between 1946 and 1954, the daughters reared in the boomer generation, had it all. The post-World War II baby boom produced the most indulged, optimistic generation of middle-class children in our nation's history. The world was our oyster. Our parents told us repeatedly that they wanted us to have all the advantages they did not have—and we did. They provided safe and comfortable homes, stressed the importance of getting an education, sent us to camp, taught us good manners and did their best to impart to us their values. Our middle class parents wanted to make sure we would be equipped to make our every dream come true, or in some cases, their every dream come true.

Yes, we had it all, or did we? Our parents did such a good job that many of us were convinced we had close to total control over our destinies. We firmly believed nothing could stop us from fulfilling our dreams. And more than anything else, we wanted to shape these dreams independently of any substantive influence from elders who had sacrificed so much in our behalf.

This book isn't about all baby boom women. It is about fifty women we interviewed, women who tried to straddle the traditions of our parents' generation and the limitless options of the Age of Aquarius. We are focusing on the women born during the first eight years of the baby boom era, the *real* baby boomers, the direct recipients of the post-war desire for stability and security. We grew and thrived in a time when the biggest news story on television might be Ike's golf score. We played hide and seek until dark and drank lemonade on summer nights on the front porch. And we made plans.

The fifty women in our study were trained for careers as professionals. They wanted to be sure that they had the ability to be independent and take care of themselves. Some focused on their careers; others saw their jobs as "something to fall back on" in case their real dream of having a family didn't pan out. The college experience of the late 60's and the early 70's influenced them—that unique time in higher education when all the rules were broken. Breaking rules would be something we would become very good at for years to come. But these women also clung to traditional values, and—in true baby boomer fashion—they pursued both tradition and change with vigor, wanting to "have it all."

The Mothers of the Boomers

The world of women in the 1940's changed dramatically. These changes created a culture that allowed women's choices to broaden. An historical, technological, and social revolution showed boomers' mothers there was more to life than tending home and children. World War II took men away from the workplace. The resulting vacuum had to be filled to support the war effort and provide for those remaining at home. Jobs previously classified for men only were reclassified, first for black men, then for single women, and finally for married women. Because women were patriotic and committed to doing their part, they took jobs outside the home. There they worked beside strangers to create goods not meant for their own families. The boundaries between men and work and women and home shattered. More significantly, women learned they could be effective outside the home.

While women were at work, they needed help with caring for children. Daycare centers opened so mothers didn't have to worry about leaving their children with no family member to care for them. The invention of the vacuum cleaner and the washing machine had simplified household tasks. Precious time could be spent doing things other than chores. TV dinners made supper easy and Tupperware saved leftovers.

Contradictions abounded over who was the ideal woman—the working girl or the sex kitten. The two most popular pin-ups illustrated the mixed messages to women. "Rosie the Riveter," with her head in a scarf, was the strong and independent worker. Betty Grable, with her beautiful hair and curvaceous body, represented the pampered woman who lived life in comfort and leisure. The messages to women: be beautiful but independent, seductive but useful, patriotic but spoiled.

The relationships between men and women, so long characterized by clear gender roles, also became complicated. Men now weren't the only ones to wear the pants in the family. Slacks and suits became acceptable attire for women as well as men. When men returned from the war, they expected their world to be as it was before. Not so. Once women experienced the possibilities and the satisfaction of multiple roles, things would never be entirely the same. Many men were not happy with this unexpected adjustment. Some even say that the baby boom was an unconscious attempt to restore the equilibrium of the past. With women at home, pregnant, maybe even barefoot, perhaps things might return to normal. And in many respects—they did. But change was inevitable. Women now had choices that gave them a taste of independence and freedom not readily available before. The opportunity to earn income and support themselves meant they could choose to marry, but not *have* to marry, in order to be cared for.

The women of the 40's were strong and hardworking. They took up the burdens of caring for their homes and families whether the men were there to help or not. Without the advantages of birth control, they willingly served the needs of their children first. Biology determined their destiny. But they saw that other things were possible for their daughters. With more and more conveniences in the home, with opportunities opening up in college and the professional schools, and with birth control putting decisions about when to begin a family in women's hands, they saw a new era of wider choices.

Following the advice of Dr. Spock, parents sacrificed to give their children every advantage. Mothers saw their daughters as capable of doing whatever they desired. If mom couldn't become a physician, her daughter certainly could. Mom would even help to make it happen. With smaller families, the finances were re-organized so that daughters as well as sons could be educated. Karen, one of the women we interviewed, remembers her mother's advice: "An education is something no one can ever take from you." Unlike property or money, a degree is forever. No stock market crash could ever steal that as it had the financial resources of the boomers' grandparents. The wisdom of these mothers shaped the vision of the baby boom generation.

The 50's—Happy Days?

Change in any form, however, does not come easily or quickly. Rapidly growing access to radio, television and the movies increased the influence the media had on women's perception of how well they were measuring up to the "ideal woman." More often than not, television trivialized the role of women, casting them in a humorous light. Consider "I Love Lucy," a popular sitcom that portrayed Lucy as an attractive, fun-loving airhead who knew her place. Whenever Lucy tried to break out of her role, it proved disastrous for her and her family. In those instances, her husband, Ricky, always bailed her out her with a very loving, but clearly condescending attitude. The series highlighted her energy and desire for a full life but left no doubt that this was best attained in the safety and security of her own home.

Again, the media were a force in maintaining the status quo, television leading the way. Young people began spending more hours in front of the tube than in school. What they saw gave them the standard against which to judge their lives. Thousands of families watched "Father Knows Best" and the "Adventures of Ozzie and Harriet" each week. The women we interviewed listed the female characters from these shows as having a big influence on their perceptions of themselves and helped them partly define the women they wanted to become.

Even Disney cartoon movies taught lessons about family life. Boomers remember the scene when Bambi's mother was killed and his father had to rescue him from the fire. Bambi's mother was depicted as a loving, nurturing, protective parent who taught Bambi how to survive in the forest. Bambi's father didn't appear early enough to save the mother and never was involved in any everyday parental responsibilities. He and his awesome antlers appear only when the exciting, spectacular, heroic rescue is necessary. As the movie ends, the cycle repeats itself, with Bambi's mate raising the little ones while he stands on a hill displaying his now awesome antlers.

Nostalgics often treasure the 50's as the best time of the twentieth century. But underlying the self-satisfaction of the decade were deepening questions about American values. This period was a time when our country confronted numerous social issues, especially race relations. Racial discrimination and desegregation became the ugly symbols for all that was still unequal in this country. How ironic and hypocritical it was. Americans had just fought a war to protect their country from the evils of Nazi Germany. We had liberated the Jews of Europe from persecution. Yet black Americans remained an oppressed minority.

This was true for middle class women as well. The major difference was that they were a protected, rather than persecuted, minority. However, protection can deny opportunity. It is noteworthy that a black woman sparked the civil rights movement. When Rosa Parks refused to go to the back of the bus, it struck a blow for equal rights, equal opportunity, equal accessibility and equal respect throughout America.

It was difficult to see female independence in most aspects of popular culture. Poodle skirts and pony tails, dances and Barbie dolls shaped the image of women. Every young girl admired the Barbie doll with her perfect body and carefully coordinated outfits that were suitable for every occasion—except work. Dick Clark hosted teen-agers who danced to the music of rock idols who entertained the non-working woman of the 50's. In the family, the father's voice was always the last word. Even a dog, Lassie, played a part in helping the woman of the house be the best wife, mother, and caretaker she could be. As in "Bambi," it was always the man of the house who rose to the occasion to protect and defend the hearth against outside dangers.

But women had not forgotten the taste of independence and self-sufficiency that came in the 40's when they worked outside the home. Serious seeds of doubt had been planted. Perhaps a woman's place was not just in the home. Maybe she could also be comfortable functioning in a more public arena, competing for jobs and opportunity even if the media presented only one accepted and socially-sanctioned option—the satisfied housewife.

While the traditional still dominated, a culture of curiosity and imagination was emerging. Science fiction literature became popular, with stories of the power of the individual to overcome his or her fate. Interstate highways made family vacations an annual event. How many boomers don't have vivid recollections of long trips to the beach or to grandmother's house in the summer in cars without air-conditioning? Travel fed the imagination. You could imagine going anywhere now. With the launching of the Explorer satellite in 1958, Americans could even imagine going literally out of this world.

An uneasiness grew as well. Though they had just won a world war, Americans began to worry about the safety and security of their nation. McCarthyism fanned fears of communism and the Russians. Anxious Americans no longer took their lifestyle for granted. Beatniks began an anti-establishment movement, sowing the seeds for the 60's assault on the status quo. Self-satisfaction was countered with questions, conservatism with independence, traditional mores with the unconventional. The stage was set for a tremendous social upheaval where rebellion would be the norm. Soon it would be "in" to be "out."

Blossoming of the Boomers

If the decades of the 40's and 50's provided the soil to nurture boomer career women, the 60's was the field in which they blossomed. Boomers left home and entered college. These were exciting times for women who were beginning to grapple with the complex task of becoming adults. Regardless of their views about their own personal lives at this point, it was hard to escape the political arena that surrounded them. The Vietnam War and the assassinations of Jack and Bobby Kennedy and Martin Luther King created an intense awareness of issues related to human rights. Many women joined movements, championing the rights of minorities, protesting injustice, and demonstrating against the war. In college, their reading went beyond the classics to controversial writers such as Nietzsche and Betty Friedan. The decision by many to attend large universities instead of small women's colleges meant more exposure to the environment of anti-establishment, rebellious feminists who were into bra burning and out of being mama's little girl.

Contradictions in College

The college experience affected these women in profound ways. In some respects it was a world of freedom and opportunity for individual discovery and expression. Those who considered professions were breaking with tradition. But they were practical and willing to work within the system to gain the opportunity to compete in the "establishment." They often felt at cross-purposes. The ultimate goal was somehow to separate from tradition, hanging onto the parts they liked while still finding ways to achieve professional positions in which they could make a difference.

The women's movement itself was not without contradictions. The message was to burn the bras but have big boobs. Be smart, but not so smart that men will be turned off. Don't be a sex object but stick to your diet and spend a fortune on white lipstick and green eye shadow.

Boomer women found little support if they broke too sharply with custom. A male friend of one of the women we interviewed asked about her plans for the years after college. When told that she was going to graduate school to pursue a doctorate, he quickly warned her not to get so much education that she couldn't get a husband. Even more surprising was the experience of another of our boomers who shared with a female counselor her dream to become a doctor. The counselor suggested that she reconsider this choice because it required many years of study. "Realistically, you probably won't be willing to do this, dear," the counselor said. She was giving this advice to a Phi Beta Kappa graduate of a leading university! These women, like others, wanted to be married and to have children. So it is not surprising that they often took this advice to heart. For the most part, they conformed to society's expectation that they should focus on traditional priorities, at least on the surface. At the same time, they were determined to fill new roles. They wanted it all. Why not be successful in the living room, the bedroom, and the board room?

The 70's

During the 70's and much of the 80's, baby boom women married and became mothers. On news channels, they watched passively the anti-establishment, anti-government movements being played out as they folded the laundry. They were concerned, but "What am I to do?" they asked themselves. After all, they had to get dinner on the table and help the children with homework. On other channels, shows bombarded them with family stories—but with new twists. "The Brady Bunch" had all the trials and triumphs of not only a family, but a blended family. This series seemed a metaphor for "All's well with the family." Ironically, outside the studio the actor who played the father in the show was neither a husband or a father. He lived instead the life of a homosexual. His ultimate death from complications from the AIDS virus symbolized again the difference between the real and the imagined culture of the time.

"Happy Days" and "All in the Family" reflected families living out traditional American values. The hit comedy "Saturday Night Live" highlighted the contradictions, the hypocrisy of daily life. We lost many of our heroes in our irreverence. Whom do we look up to after Watergate? We found solace in such films as "Star Wars," which gave us a fantasy world with nonhuman heroes to admire. We saw the strong woman in leadership, the mercenary man, the gentle warrior, the wise teacher, and other prototypes we seemed to have difficulty finding in real life.

The 80's and 90's

The social turbulence of the 70's gave way to the excesses of the 80's. As boomer women tried to rear children, go to work each day, and preserve their marriages (not always in that order), the 80's were a time of intensity and pressure. Perhaps the focus on "me" was a way to survive the swirling waters of change and chaos. There seemed to be just too much of everything. Too many TV channels. Too much to buy. Too much emphasis on status. Too much violence in and out of homes. No longer could we trust all good things to come of our creations. AIDS meant that free love wasn't so free after all. Toxic Shock Syndrome meant that the freedom and comfort of tampons must be balanced against complications that could kill you. The sky was the limit for women but, as we learned so visibly when Christa McAuliffe lost her life in the explosion of the Challenger, it wasn't always without costs. Women could run for high government office, even president. Geraldine Ferraro's failure made it clear voters weren't ready for a woman just as aggressive as a man.

Women were earning more advanced degrees in colleges than ever before. But as they entered male-dominated professions, there were criticisms from within the professions and attacks from without. It became apparent to many that they would have to work twice as hard as a man and be twice as smart to be thought half as good.

During the 90's, many women reached higher levels of successes but realized that perhaps they couldn't have it all. Or maybe having it all meant something different from what they had first envisioned. Their parents were entering old age and some of their friends were suffering from illness and early death. They knew as never before that life is fragile and fleeting. They began to examine the meaning of their lives and question how they were spending their time.

Now they face the fifth decade with a broad range of experiences, some successful, some not so successful. They find themselves in a world changing so rapidly that the greatest tool for survival is simply knowing how to cope with change. What now? Do they enter the last phase of their career and their upcoming retirement in the same way as men? Do the same drives that led them to seek "superwoman" status when they were younger now make them want to work longer, work differently, or not work at all? What of relationships—with husband, children, parents, and friends? How do their talents and interests fit with the needs of the larger community?

We are still our mothers' daughters and they taught us well. Just as they handled the contradictions of their time, so, too, will we. Managing constant change, negotiating countless choices and handling ever-present contradictions will simply remain as three regular items on the "to do" list. Based on the responses of our boomer women—No problem!

Chapter 2

WHO ARE WE AT FIFTY?

Wᴴᴼ are we? Although the women we interviewed intensively numbered only fifty, their lives encompassed a remarkable variety of experiences. They lived and attended college in twenty-five states spread across several regions of the United States. Most have traveled abroad, and some also lived or studied in foreign countries. Only nine have never left their home state. They took a wide variety of career paths, some having as many as eight different full-time jobs over the years. Armed with solid educational backgrounds, they represent 35 professions. More than a third of those we interviewed hold doctoral or medical degrees, another third have a masters', and one fifth have bachelors' degrees. The remaining had some higher education beyond high school, most completing specialist degrees.

We had every kind of marital status represented in our group. Seventy-eight percent were married and seven percent were divorced. The rest were widowed or had always been single. Most had reared children or stepchildren; some had none. Eighty-four percent were white and sixteen percent were African-American.

Diverse as these women were, we found that their experiences revolved around four themes—career, family, friendships and personal goals. Careers were vitally important to them. Yet for most, family remained paramount. Friendships were also important and connected them to other women in enduring ways. Finally, for all these baby boomers, personal goals—goals embracing health, hope, and spirituality—are a defining characteristic. Understanding these themes helps us recognize a group of women who have carved out new paths, while holding on to key traditions. By blending change and tradition, these middle-class baby boomers have attempted to have everything. And if their degree of happiness in life is any indication, they have succeeded.

Career

"I want to grow up to be a great woman . . . . just like dad."

At some time, all the baby boomers interviewed for this book pursued a career. Most are still working in some capacity and remain very happy with the career choices they made. On a scale ranging from one to ten (with 10 being the most satisfied), they gave themselves an average score of 8.1 in overall satisfaction with their careers. Nearly two-thirds rated their satisfaction as 8 or higher. These are remarkably high scores. Obviously career has been important and deeply rewarding.

Just as compelling is the fact that the baby boomers have been breaking new ground in their careers. A majority of the thirty-five professions that they pursued during the last three decades would have been considered jobs for men in their mother's generation. In the 1950's, when the baby boomers were determining a course for themselves, there were few female role models for such professions as college professor, physician, real estate agent, business owner, and minister. Yet they moved into unfamiliar territory and made it comfortable and rewarding.

Despite being work-oriented and being seen as too ambitious by some, most have not allowed work to dominate their lives. Half of those interviewed said that their family is and has always been their highest priority. For another forty percent, work and family have had equal priority over the course of time. Work and home priorities may have shifted for them, depending on what was happening during certain times. For example, when the baby boomers' children were young, work often had to take a backseat, and when some went through divorces, work again became more important. Only ten percent said that work had always been their highest priority.

What has made their work so meaningful to them? This group of women finds the most rewarding aspects of work in their dealings with people and with relationships. Combining traditional values and change, they held onto typically "feminine" concerns while pioneering in new areas of the workforce. Two-thirds of the women said that helping people to grow, mentoring others at work, and enabling groups or individuals to meet their goals and achieve success gave them the most pleasure when on the job. While pursuing a career, these women remained nurturers. Their presence changed the workplace, but they did not let the workplace change them.

These women also regard their own personal growth as critical to seeing their jobs as valuable. Several described specific situations that caused them to leave positions because opportunities for growth were lacking. In the words of one, "I was going nowhere. I was bored and needed stimulation." Many also wanted to feel needed and appreciated by the people and organizations in which they work. In the words of a boomer who felt appreciated, "When I won 'Top Salesperson of the Year,' I knew then they could see what I had done." Another who did not said, "I probably would not have left that job except for the fact that no one asked me to stay. How important to them could I have been?"

Interestingly, as successful as they have been as a group and as satisfied as they say they are with their vocational paths, almost one-third claimed that they would choose a completely different career if they had it to do over. Another quarter said that they would stay in the same general fields, but would change their position in them. "I probably would have still been a teacher," one told us, "but I would have pursued a doctorate so that I could teach in college." Said another, "I would still choose medicine, but I would rather have been a physician than a nurse." Only twenty-five percent said that they would make exactly the same decisions about their career. For most, years of successful work have not diminished their craving for a new challenge.

This is a group of achievers who want to do everything well, and doing everything well can be stressful. When asked what the most stressful parts of their careers had been, the most frequent response was "not being able to get it all done." They worried about meeting deadlines, keeping long hours, having too many outside responsibilities to juggle at once—especially when trying to raise a family. "I wanted to be a great mother and a great business woman," said one. "I had to settle for either being 'good' at both or 'great' in one and 'so-so' in the other."

Adding to their stress was working for incompetent bosses, "inept administrators," or "having no support from small-minded superiors." Often these circumstances were present in settings where they had no control. "I rarely had input into my responsibilities or how they were to be carried out," said one. "They were simply assigned to me." Another said, "I can't tell you how many nights I went home with a headache after a day of working for a complete idiot!" The pressures are not always someone else's fault, however. Almost ten percent of the women admitted that most of their stress was self-imposed. For example, one said, "My lack of ability to be flexible made everything worse for me." Others confessed, "I tried to do too much and please too many people."

As they moved into the workforce, these women were often on their own. In discussing their careers, a clear majority (62%) stated that they had no professional role models. When they could identify someone who gave them advice, it was usually a man—especially in the male-dominated fields with few or no women. According to one, "I found that the best way to learn was to watch the men and design some way that would work for me to do what they did. It was usually trial and error."

Some did identify role models, however. One fifth of our boomers said they had significant role models for their career, people who took a serious interest in their development and success. These role models were usually their bosses, professors in college, or teachers who had made an impact on them. Several of the women said that colleagues and family members were also important to them in this way as well. "Even though my mother was never a real estate agent, her instincts about people have been the best source of guidance for me, especially when I started out," one pointed out. "She has taught me how to handle myself in every situation all through my career."

As accomplished as these women are professionally, they are also very hard on themselves. Asked what their biggest sources of disappointment were in their careers, most (about 40%) reflected that it was in their own abilities or in their performance. Typical responses: "I wasn't able to handle the work load" or "I needed to be more aggressive—I allowed them to roll over me" or "I should have changed jobs earlier" or "I should have finished my education." In the same breath the women felt a lack of respect for their work. "I got no support or respect." "My work has never been formally recognized." "I didn't get the promotion I deserved."

"Okay, so did you feel lonely and isolated in your work?" we asked them. To our surprise, we discovered that they were pretty evenly divided. Roughly a third said that they were "very isolated," but just as many said they weren't and the rest gave us a middling response. In conversations it became clear that the degree of isolation in the workplace related to the type of job someone had and whether that job lent itself to interacting with others. For example, teachers in the study rarely felt isolated, whereas, sales representatives often did. How people interpret the word "lonely" is also important. One woman said she felt "very isolated"—but explained that she interpreted the phrase as meaning "alone," and even values time by herself. She added, "Giving myself [that rating] is a good thing. Years ago, I might have said 'in the middle' because I was always trying to be included and aimed to be around people as much as possible. I've actually worked hard to let some of that need go."

Family

"What is important is all relative."

Despite the importance of career, the women we studied said their families are *the* most important part of their lives. With clear ideas of the value of family, it was no surprise that approximately forty-two percent of the women said they would change almost nothing about the way they dealt with their families through the years. Said one busy therapist, "I made sure that no matter what was on the list for that day, my children were taken care of—if not by my husband or me, then by relatives." Another said, "I wouldn't change a thing. When the first thought you have every morning for twenty years is 'What do I need to do for my kids today?' then you don't look back. I did the best I could."

For those with children, motherhood dominates. One-third discussed changes they would make that related to their children. Several who had no children of their own said that, if they could do it again, they would adopt children. On the other hand, two of the women who had adopted children said they would not repeat that decision if they could do it over. Others said they would have waited until later to marry and start a family. Many indicated that they would be with their children more, playing, traveling, and just "spending more quality time with them."

Some said they would change the way they had behaved with other family members. For example, one wished she had spoken up more about tension with her parents. "Instead of trying to keep everybody happy, I should have been less afraid of hurting someone's feelings. I've been angry for years over things that I should have gotten straightened out earlier." Another said she would have tried harder to understand and get to know her brothers. "We've missed out on so much time together. I don't even know my nieces."

Money wasn't a concern. Who controls it in a family can be complicated and often cause a divorce. But few of the women we interviewed had problems with it. Slightly more than half of these women managed the money in their families. Here again, they were combining tradition and new roles. The husband managed the money in only a fifth of these households, and in the remainder, both wife and husband shared that responsibility. In the shared situations, some women reported that they paid the bills while their husbands managed the investments. Most of these women said, however, that husband and wife make decisions together about major purchases. Only a few said that they had completely separate accounts. Or as one boomer said, "I handle MY money and he manages OUR money."

Twenty-seven percent of the women we interviewed had no biological children, although many did have stepchildren. For those who had children, we were very interested in how they perceive themselves as parents. We assumed that, as baby boomers, they might have completely different (and better) ways of going about raising children from their parents. We asked them if they considered themselves better parents compared to their mothers. More than half agreed (often strongly) that they were better parents. One said, "I think I have given my children more attention than I got. I also listen to them better than she listened to me." Less than a quarter thought their mothers were better parents, while the rest weren't sure. A typical response for the last group: "I really can't say. There are ways I am better and there are ways she was better."

When we asked the same question regarding their fathers,

the women were even more adamant. Fully three-quarters agreed (and strongly) that they were better parents than Dad. One said, "He was never home and when he was, Mom still did everything for us." Another said, "He was a good dad, but didn't try very hard to understand me."

The women feel strongly their family life is better for their working outside the home. Over ninety percent disagreed that their family life would have been happier had they not chosen to work. Many said they would not be the people they were if they hadn't had a career. One said her family would have suffered if "all of her 'emotional eggs' related to her sense of worth and accomplishment had been in the family basket." Likewise, almost all of them rejected the notion that their relationships with their husbands would have been better if they had no career. One did say it was possible that her HUSBAND might have been happier, but she wouldn't have been. So the relationship would have suffered. "If I'm not happy, no one's happy!"

Our women believe they worked hard to always be there for their families. When we asked whether commitments at work made it difficult to be available for their families, sixty percent disagreed. The other forty percent felt that there were many times when their work made it hard to be home when needed. "I remember once when I couldn't leave work when my son got sick," one recalled. "I telephoned my husband, two neighbors and a friend from church, but no one was home. I was frantic. Finally, the school nurse who was scheduled to be at another location agreed to take care of him for several hours till I could get away. I felt so guilty."

Friendships

"How about going to the beach with me? I feel like being alone."

Friendships were one of the most important and complicated issues these women discussed. Contact with other women has remained extremely important to them and there is no underestimating the value they place on special friends with whom they can totally relax and be themselves. Sometimes finding time to maintain old friendships or make new ones was difficult, but most managed to stay in touch with those most important to them. However, it was evident that this had taken a back seat for many—not by choice but by necessity. These busy women found that they had to put first things first— and "first things" were usually family and career.

Asked if they missed the connections with friends outside the workplace, over a third said "yes" and over one fifth said "sometimes." But the rest said they, in fact, worked hard to maintain those contacts. Said one, "My best friends are like extended family and I include them in my plans as much as possible. I can't be without them." While they would like occasional opportunities to go somewhere with a friend, many said that the need for "girl talk" could be met in phone conversations or over lunch, rather than the daylong outings or weekend excursions they used to plan. "I find that I have to make a concerted effort to get them on my calendar at all. They are at least as important to me as any business appointment. But it's worth it to me." On the other hand, one said, "As I get older, I find that I have become my own best friend."

When we asked them whether their friends tended not to include them in their plans because they perceived them as too busy, the women were evenly divided. Whichever way they responded, there were a surprising number who shared the sentiments of one of our boomers: "Most of my friends are working and have families like I do. I don't hesitate to call her because I think she's too busy—I just gamble that she might be free. Sometimes it works and other times it doesn't. She does the same where I am concerned."

These baby boomers understand the value of friendships and don't plan to miss out on these significant connections with other women. Most of them are also "women's women."

All of those we interviewed except two said that they have more women than men friends, and almost half said they have more friends than they can give proper attention to. As one put it, "It's not that friends aren't in my life, it's more that I simply can't keep up with all of them. And what's worse, I keep meeting interesting people that I wish I had the time to get to know." Almost the same percentage said they have just the right number of friends at this time. Far fewer said they didn't have enough friends. "I have lots of 'acquaintances,'" said one, "but I need more true friends."

These women are also very specific about the qualities they want in their friends. No one hesitated to provide a list of usually three to four characteristics they found essential. The most frequently mentioned was the ability of the friend to "accept" her as she was and to be honest and a good listener. One said, "Friendships are the light in the dark of life to me. If I can't get honest feedback from someone who loves and accepts me for who I am, then there is no point in talking to her." These women also want someone who is loyal, trustworthy and shares the same values. It was also important to have common interests, for the friends to "be there" for them, and be fun loving. In the words of one, "I have to be able to laugh. My favorite friends find the same things funny that I do. I think it's a true gauge of similar attitudes about life."

Personal Goals for Body and Soul

"It's a Fact: Clothes Shrink if Left in a Closet During the Winter."

Perhaps not surprisingly, these active women put a high priority on physical fitness. Three fourths said that they have a daily exercise regimen or work out at least three to five days a week. Most of the rest said they exercise sporadically, with only a few saying they do nothing. Two thirds of the women said that walking is their primary activity. This is understandable because it's something these busy women can do anytime with anyone or by themselves. In much smaller numbers, the others reported lifting weights, doing aerobic exercise, playing tennis, swimming, biking, golfing, dancing, using the treadmill, or working in the yard.

Many are involved in several sports and exercise activities. "I just make sure I do something every day and that 'something' will vary," said one. Many are members of sports clubs and some even work out with trainers. Almost everyone we interviewed mentioned her diet in some way, most saying they try to watch carefully what they eat. Others, however, honestly admitted that they have "bad" eating habits and need to pay better attention. One confessed, "I am usually so busy at work that I have fallen into the habit of eating fast food for lunch most days a week. It's catching up with me and trying to lose these last fifteen pounds is going to be very hard."

To these women, mental and spiritual health are as essential as physical well being. When we asked the boomers what inspired them, we learned that spiritual renewal is far from an afterthought. One quickly said, "SO many things." This group reads a lot, especially good novels, literature and poetry. One boomer said, "I love to lose myself in books—especially ones about other places I haven't visited or about ordinary people who do extraordinary things." Relationships with friends and special people also inspired them. One said, "Nothing gives me more hope on a bad day than to watch my children at play." Another said, "I am always uplifted by a good conversation with my best friend." Many claimed that nature was their greatest source of inspiration,—a beautiful sunset or the grandeur of mountains. Some also said seeing people succeed and being around good people gave them a boost. Others commented that family, hard work, music, and travel stimulated them.

But far and away the biggest source of inspiration was spiritual. Almost one third of the women listed some aspect of their individual spiritual journeys as the key to their well-being. Many said that reading the Bible, participating in Bible study groups, praying, or being involved in church was their single biggest source of peace and hope. Four out of every five of the women belong to a church or synagogue and most said they attended regularly. They represented 10 different religious affiliations. Most describe themselves as "spiritual." Only one said she did not consider herself a spiritual person at all. In fact, she added, "I can't think of anything or anyone who 'inspires' me."

Satisfaction with Life

"How sweet it is"

The boomers did not choose the familiar. They tried to blend traditional values with new roles and aspirations. They sought new ways of doing things. Venturing into unknown social territory was neither easy nor safe, and the demands on their time could be stressful or isolating. Thus, it was natural to wonder how they felt—at fifty—about the choices they had made. Had they chosen wisely?

The best news from our hours of conversation with these boomers is that they are extremely satisfied with their lives as a whole. An amazing eighty-eight percent claim to be very satisfied. Most described feeling very fortunate, both personally and professionally. They were happy for the fact that they had resources to deal with adversity when bad times occurred. For example, one boomer said, "I've had some hard knocks, but someone was always there to help me. I've been blessed."

These women had dreams of how they wanted their lives to be. Comparing these dreams to the way things have turned out so far, three quarters say that their lives were close to their ideal: "I wanted to have a family and a career. I thought teaching would let me have both—and it has. Both my daughters now want to teach also and that makes me feel that they think I did well. After all, imitation is the sincerest form of flattery, right?" Another woman said, "When I was in college,

I promised myself that I would be important and that people would know who I was. I don't know if I am 'important,' but I am well-known nationally for my writing. It's exactly what I envisioned."

An overwhelming majority also reports that the conditions of their lives are excellent and they have the important things in life that they want. For most, these important things include having a comfortable place to live, meaningful work, fulfilling relationships, and financial security. For some, it means the hope of having those things and the feeling that those things will occur for them. In the words of one, "I do believe that my conditions are excellent. Even though I struggle daily to have the basics, I do somehow manage to have them. I am sure that, if I continue to save and plan, things will get easier."

As satisfied as this group claims to be, we wondered if they would change any thing about their lives if they had the chance. Almost two-thirds said they wouldn't. The others, however, do say they would make some changes. What they would change varied. Some said that they would go into a different career, others said they would have children. Still others said that they would live in a different part of the country. We asked them if they were happy with the way they balanced career, family and personal needs over the years. As hard as that was sometimes to do, practically all said they were. One boomer's response summarized many of the ones we heard: "I wanted it all— career and family—and I worked my butt off every day to make sure everything I considered important was done. I made myself stop work in time to get dinner on the table and get my daughter to Scouts. I even gave up a few promotions that meant I would have to travel more. I also expected my family to help out when I was meeting a deadline. I admit that keeping my personal needs in the mix was a challenge and I probably could have done better on that one. But considering everything, I did okay."

They made it. These girls who made careful plans and dreamed of possibilities when they were young have "arrived."

And most did it without role models. We asked them who their role models were for the kind of life they wanted to lead. Just as they had no professional role models, a majority said they had no life role models. Most of those agreed with one woman who said, "I can't think of anyone who had the kind of life I wanted." Another said, "I created my life as much out of what I saw and didn't like as anything else. I just decided to do things differently." Others created a "composite" life out of the parts they liked in several people.

Still, some did identify role models, naming their mothers, grandmothers, and husbands, teachers, or friends. Whether they followed someone else's lead or followed their own hearts, this group is one that has clearly come into its own. These baby boom women are happy, satisfied and successful members of society, people who, at least at this point, are winning the "game of life."

PART II

CHOOSING A GAME PLAN

Chapter 3

THE TYPES OF BABY BOOM WOMEN AT FIFTY

The Choices We Made

WHEN the baby boomers were growing up in the 1950's, they had three choices of ice cream—vanilla, chocolate, and strawberry. By the time they were in high school, Howard Johnson's had 28 flavors. As college graduates, there were even more. So many choices! These women responded in different ways to these new options. Most loved having so much to pick from, amusing themselves by examining the many delicious possibilities, looking for the very best flavor. Others found the many choices mind-boggling. They stared at all those tubs of ice cream in the freezer immobilized. Finally, in frustration, they either resorted to one of the old, familiar flavors, gambled with something new, or, if really desperate, let someone else pick it for them.

This explosion of options available to them was characteristic of the generation. And what made things worse (or better, depending on your point of view) was that the many new options weren't limited to ice cream; there was more to choose in every part of their lives as well. With the women's liberation movement, boomer women now had doors opened professionally that had previously been closed. They knew all too well that people are both the determiners and the products of their choices, so these "opportunities" sometimes felt like new and heavy burdens. They naturally wanted to make the right decisions; so learning even how to make these choices was, in itself, a new experience.

Some of the choices were not difficult and not particularly different from those of their mothers. These included the familiar questions of whether or not to go to college, and if so, where. Once there, what should they major in? How far from home should they venture? Other choices, however, were new for them, and the most important for many was that of career. While a majority were still comfortable choosing teaching, nursing or office work, many considered the new opportunities now available. At the same time, other complex social questions arose for them, such as the issue of sex. The pill made this decision both easier and much more complicated than ever before. Should they marry? Should they have children? If so, when? For baby boomer women the decisions to be made were exciting, scary and endless.

Suddenly faced with so many choices, they responded not unlike they did at the ice cream parlor. Some embraced the many new options, determined to try them all. They would experiment with "a new flavor," curious about what pleasure or distaste it might bring. Many strived to become "superwomen" who would try as many flavors as possible, maybe even inventing one of their own. They relished the chance to blaze new trails on the career front, perhaps also to marry wonderful men who would be perfect companions for them and fathers for their children, to maintain beautiful homes, friendships and community involvements, and still be a size 6.

Others, daunted by the overwhelming number of choices, found making the decisions difficult. They were often reluctant to make choices at all, preferring, "to keep their options open." In many situations, these women were even happier when other people or external circumstances made the decisions for them. When they did this, they tended to think, as one boomer said, that they were being "laid back, preferring to consider the desires and needs of others, or simply being willing to take life as it comes." They also felt that making a choice closed a door to the other choices. What if something better were to come up the next day?

Of course, the decision not to make a choice is a choice in itself. Like it or not, life forces everyone into some direction whether one wills it or not. It's just a matter of whether people want to be the masters of their own fate, trying to control things to the extent they can or to let other people and circumstances do that for them. The choices individuals make create their own realities.

Like all people, the women we interviewed have made choices in a variety of ways and for many reasons. Some tended to make them quickly, confident that they can always make another choice if they want to change something. Others took their time, feeling that making a decision is a heavy burden and that all possibilities must be weighed carefully. The stories these women tell illustrate the outcomes of these choices and the ways in which they chose to make them.

Circumstances shape choices. So do the temperament and personality of the chooser. Sometimes circumstances determine one's path, but individuals also have choices in terms of how they handle circumstances. For example, several of the women we interviewed reported that their dreams in college were basically to get married and have a family. Any career aspirations were secondary to that goal—interesting perhaps— but not a main focus in their lives. However, our boomers found themselves making different decisions about their careers when they didn't marry at all, or when they married and divorced. In some cases, circumstances eventually forced them to pursue career paths that would provide for more financial security. These careers would also become an important source of personal gratification, as important as their families. One said, "I never wanted to run a business, it just became necessary if I was to take care of myself. Now it is my life's blood and also gives me more overall satisfaction than I ever thought a job could. It is a rare that I consider a day complete unless I do something related to my work."

The most important factor that affects any decision one makes, however, is the issue of "baggage." All of us bring to every situation experiences and messages from significant others that define how we think of ourselves. Some baggage is "good," affirming us and encouraging us to make decisions that will result in more positive feelings. Cindy chooses the beach for most of her vacations. "As a child," she says, "the beach was the one place our family spent every summer just being together and having fun. Even now, I associate such times with feeling secure, loved and relaxed."

Baggage can also be "bad," triggering efforts to avoid unpleasant experiences and negative feelings. Loretta refuses to fly because as a teen-ager turbulence forced her plane to land in a cornfield. Powerful emotions such as the need for self-protection and self-esteem affect how we make important and routine choices daily. Ego is involved when a woman chooses to buy an expensive car because it provides status or to marry someone her parents dislike to flaunt her independence or to buy a dress because it makes her look thin.

One boomer, Lou, learned that her job would probably disappear because of company downsizing. She had worked hard to earn her position as supervisor in a highly visible department. She loved her job and enjoyed the respect and sense of achievement it provided. She was the only child of two hardworking parents who had little money. They took on double shifts with low wages to afford everything she needed and even sent her to an elite private college. She was the light of their lives, the symbol of their success. She felt a certain amount of pressure to "make them proud." Regardless of how difficult it had been for them at times, they made sure she was safe, loved, and had everything she needed, almost to the point of being overprotective. Her promotion to this job was the symbol that all of her efforts and those of her parents had paid off.

Soon after Lou heard of possible changes at the company, she was offered another excellent position in a neighboring city where she preferred not to live. She had several options— take the new job, begin an active job search, or wait things out and hope that the rumor wasn't true. She selected "Door Number 3." She wanted to keep her job, not only for herself, but also for her parents. The overall benefits to her self-esteem and pride seemed worth the gamble. Unfortunately for her, the rumor was true. She ended up unemployed for almost nine months before accepting a lesser position.

This choice is typical of Lou's approach to handling major decisions. She ignores negative possibilities. She has an upbeat personality, is very friendly and is always positive about everything and everybody. Her friends describe her as a joy, but also naïve about the world. Said one, "She doesn't look at the facts if they are unpleasant. She always hopes for the best and seems really surprised when things turn out badly. It has happened more times than I can count. She comes across as someone who needs to be taken care of and trusts that her friends, boyfriends or bosses will always act in her best interest." This situation is an example of a choice determined by circumstances, the boomer's temperament, and baggage from her past. She assumes that "things will turn out for me, they always do." That was her approach to life.

Each woman we interviewed had a unique approach to life. But we discovered seven patterns in the approaches the women took. Likewise, we noticed that each group's approach was very much like that of the athletes in particular sports. So we identified seven types of women who closely correspond to seven different sports. The women in each type shared a common goal with the athletes in each of the sports—they all want to "win," either at a game or at the "game of life." They all develop a "game plan" to win. And once they identify a "game plan" that seems to work, they usually can't change it any more easily than they can change who they are.

Each type loosely reflects personality factors in the baby

boom women we interviewed, coupled with general patterns related to choices they made. Just as some sports are familiar and traditional, some of our women followed conventional lives like their mothers. They made "safe" choices that allowed them to be feminine, nurturing, and keepers of the home. But just as some sports are more unusual, the life decisions other women made were very unconventional. They broke the rules, tried new and risky approaches to life, and created a very different definition of success for "the new woman."

The next chapters will discuss the seven sports-related types of women in more detail. If you put the women and the sports they represent on a scale—with conventional at one end and unconventional at the other—it would look like this:

Approaches to Life of Baby Boom Women

Cheerleader Baseball Player Lap Swimmer Sailor Martial Artist Mountain Climber Distance Runner

Conventional _____ Unconventional

Women on the "conventional" end of the scale approach life similar to what might have been expected from our parents' generation. The "Cheerleaders" make support of their families the center of their lives. The "Baseball Players" nurture others in both their career choices and in making home a priority. Lap swimmers choose lifestyles that allow them to maintain routines.

Women on the "unconventional" end of the scale are the most independent in terms of making life choices that are different from the norm. Distance runners follow their own paths, regardless of society's expectations. Mountain Climbers are risk-takers, identifying goals that many have not attempted before and are relentless in their pursuit of the peak. Martial Artists are the women who are advocates for people and causes.

Sailors are the middle—women who take the best of both the traditional world of their mothers and the new options available to them as they came of age.

Women in each group shared the same approach to life regardless of the careers they chose, their marital status, or whether or not they had children. For each type, the only consideration was general approach to life. This surprised us most with respect to the particular professions the women chose. We assumed that women in similar professions would fall into the same types. Not always true. For example, a teacher might be a baseball player but could just as easily be a lap swimmer, a mountain climber, a distance runner, or any other type on the scale. We found that women in a particular group thought about things and reacted to situations in the same way. But within each type, we also identified extremes. For example, "Mountain Climbers" could be driven workaholics, determined to meet their goals at all costs, grimly fighting any obstacles that may arise. Or they were creative entrepreneurs who enjoy the climb, who aim for the top, but are more relaxed about the obstacles that may arise. They even look for ways to use the obstacles as part of the plan to meet their goals. Typically, most "Mountain Climbers" fall somewhere between the two extremes.

Of course, no woman falls neatly into one of these groups. You could be a "Cheerleader" during one phase of your life and a "Martial Artist" in another. The choices these women have made along the way reflect what they value, what they want, and how they think about solving problems they have faced. Their approaches to the game of life reflect their personalities and how they have chosen to interpret their circumstances.

Chapter 4

THE CHEERLEADER

"From Barbies to Barbells"

SHELIA raced through her house to find the list of errands that had to be completed before the afternoon was over. She still had to shop for food for the dinner party she was hosting for her husband's boss that evening, pick up shirts from the cleaners, mail college applications for her son, and drive her daughter Beth to cheerleading practice by 4:00p.m. As if there weren't enough things already on the list for the afternoon, she would somehow have to return Beth to school for another function by 6:00p.m.

But by the time she reached the 4:00 p.m. practice, she considered it a break. She never minded going to practice and watching her daughter and did so whenever she had a chance. Beth had worked hard to become captain of the cheerleading squad and was thriving as the leader. Shelia watched and held her breath as Beth mobilized her teammates into a difficult and potentially dangerous pyramid formation. She admired Beth's physical strength, her ability as an outstanding athlete and an excellent student, as well as the self-confidence that she had developed over the years. "How different things are for young women in the 1990's," Shelia thought. What she wouldn't have done to feel that empowered when she was that age!

Shelia remembered her own dream to be a cheerleader when she was growing up. When she was in high school in the 1960's, she used to look forward to Friday night football games with her friends. She went primarily to visit and enjoy the band and other parts of the "show." She understood the rules of the game and sometimes even watched parts of it, but mostly, like many others in the stands, she was fascinated with the cheerleaders. It seemed they were always the prettiest, the most popular and the most successful—the envy of most of the girls in her school. As everyone watched, they performed their carefully orchestrated routines with the precision of the Rockettes at Radio City Music Hall. Along the sidelines, even little girls as young as 6 or 7 imitated them.

Shelia smiled as she remembered trying out for the squad each year then being so disappointed when she never made the cut. She spent hours practicing in her backyard or in her room doing the cheers in front of a mirror and smiling at imaginary crowds. She loved her world at school and, like most teen-agers, wanted more than anything to fit in. But more importantly, she also wanted to be special, someone everyone would look up to. In her school, that meant being a cheerleader and everyone knew that only the best would be selected. How she used to worry that she would never make it! But today, as she watched her daughter's team master another unbelievable stunt, she came to the realization that she, in fact, had made it. At this point in her life and in the truest sense of the word, she was indeed the consummate cheerleader.

Professional Wife

Women in this group have made the needs and ultimately the happiness of the ones they love the focus of their lives. While all were prepared for a career, they see their real jobs as that of "professional wives," a term that can be interpreted in two ways, both putting the emphasis on the word "wife." Some of the women in this group are professionals in their own right but they tend to fit job requirements around the more important needs of their families. Others are actually full-time wives who see their home responsibilities as their "profession." Regardless, they all have made a conscious decision to define as their basic mission the support and success of their husbands and children. Typically, they are the wives of corporate executives, ministers, men in the military, politicians or any of the many other professions that most require a "cheerleader" along the sidelines.

As athletes, cheerleaders have the same role with the teams they support. On the squads, they must be prepared to perform one of three functions assigned to them on the basis of their skills and strengths. A cheerleader will either be a "base," a "spotter," or a "flyer." Similarly, our baby boom cheerleaders manage not only to do all three functions, but also to do them regularly and with finesse. First, "bases" are always the strong support of the squad, the ones who can be counted on to hold up the other girls as they complete a formation. They must be strong and able to withstand the weight of the rest of the group. Baby boom cheerleaders do the same for their families, always being the ones who can be counted on to be the strength and solid foundation for everyone else.

Claire has always been Phil's base. When they dated in college, she often helped him with his courses and offered suggestions when he needed to make important decisions about his future. Acting on her wise suggestions, he has become an extremely successful corporate executive and credits her constant support and input as a key to his success. Even now, she continues to make many of the decisions about their lives, including raising the children, running the household, and paying the bills.

Spotters have the task of making sure no one falls or gets hurt as the others go through their routines in practices or during games. They are always present when needed and ready to help if someone does slip. Likewise, these wives and mothers make it their business to be constantly on the lookout for danger or trouble when it might affect their husbands or children. They're always lending a helpful hand or providing a timely "Be careful, watch your step there" whenever it seems necessary. If someone does fall, (lose a big account or promotion), they are the first ones to be on the scene with TLC, chicken soup or whatever seems to work. Several women in this group said that they usually are the ones who most often see potential problems ahead in the lives of their family. One said, "I often hear, 'Mom, you were right again. When will I learn to listen?'"

Sometimes, there are rewards. While they spend most of their time behind the scenes, occasions arise when they are on pedestals and they are recognized for what they do. They are like the flyers on the cheerleading squads, figuratively arching their backs and perching proudly high above everyone. For Amy's fiftieth birthday, her husband Sam organized and pulled off a fabulous surprise party. He had contacted friends in other states as well as all of her close friends nearby. He hired special caterers, a magician for entertainment, and had every detail covered. He wanted it to be *her* day, a day when everyone she usually takes care of in some way could honor her for how special she is to them.

It's true that in the extreme, women in this group can be either completely dependent on their husbands for all important matters or the real power behind the scenes. Those "cheerleaders" who do the minimum in terms of actively participating in the lives of the family may sit passively by and serve as ornaments for their husbands. They have no desire for real involvement and silently support their husbands and children in the background. They show up to events and bring refreshments, but keep quiet in most situations.

On the other hand, some cheerleaders are the true power behind the scenes. They know how to play their role as cheerleader, but they also know how he should play his role. These women are often both smarter than their husbands and have a deeper understanding of what needs to be done and how it should be done. They cheer loudly for their families in public, but also "advise" them even more loudly at home. Most cheerleaders fall somewhere in between the two extremes.

Girls or Women?

Girls in the 1960's didn't typically play high profile, competitive sports. Yes, most schools had an array of athletic options for girls—tennis, basketball, etc. and of course cheerleading, although many debated whether or not it was a true sport. Attitudes towards those who participated in the "sport" of cheerleading ranged from respect to resentment. Granted, no one denied that it took hours to perfect and create routines that took energy and work. But to those who felt that it wasn't a legitimate sport, it seemed that it was more a glorified pep club organized for girls who sought popularity and attention. You even heard cheerleader jokes, like the "dumb blond" jokes of the 1990's.

Things have changed in the sport of cheerleading— especially the qualifications for being one. Yesteryear's cheerleader had to be pretty and well liked, an attractive diversion to the *real* game. You had to know the rules of the game but not be an expert. Rooting for the team was a lightweight activity that girls, not women, performed. In fact, girls then weren't encouraged to do much of anything that might be perceived as unfeminine. With finding a date for the dance the most popular pastime, one definitely had to be feminine.

Not today. Cheerleading, along with every other sport females join in increasing numbers, is for WOMEN! Competition is keen. The exercise and training for today's cheerleaders rival any sport. College cheerleaders have had years of formal training as gymnasts and the number of cheerleading schools and academies has increased dramatically. By the time these women reach the college level, they are regularly performing death-defying acrobatics that astound crowds.

This sport is not for the faint-hearted; rather it is for gymnasts who are true athletes. Similarly, baby boom cheerleaders often face overwhelming demands in the course of their daily routines that require more of them than the cheerleaders their mother's generation could possibly imagine. Today, the average college cheerleader practices six to seven hours a day, which, in addition to the routines, includes weight lifting, running and rigorous physical conditioning. Many colleges now even offer scholarships for cheerleading, and championship competitions are held at the state, regional and national levels. Just as men have seen athletics as a stepping stone to making their dreams come true, many women have found the same option available through cheerleading. It is no coincidence that sometime during the last decade, high school yearbooks began replacing captions labeled Girl's Sports with Women's Sports.

My Husband/Myself

All of the women interviewed in this group were married and had children. They often had spent their lives behind the scenes "cheering" for their husbands and children, creating and maintaining a comfortable home environment that served as a base of security from which their families could excel in the world. Some even held a full-time or part-time job themselves, but all readily indicated that their husband and children are their primary focus and have been so from the beginning. The role of wife and mother was included in their plan to have it all. They believe that if their husband is successful, they are successful, just as when the team is winning, the cheerleader is winning. The best part, and ultimately the goal, of this approach is that the cheerleader gets to share the successes she'll help her husband achieve, enjoying her role as wife and mother as part of the package.

Shelia quoted her daughter as saying that the longer the cheerleading squad is together, the more its members become parts of one body—one unit. When they are performing a stunt, one instinctively reaches out for an arm, a leg, or whatever part of the "body" is needed to complete the move or to stop a fall. Shelia feels that this very much describes her relationship with her husband. The longer they are together, the more and more they are part of a unified entity that moves in tandem to meet the demands of their lives.

The cheerleader and her husband are true partners in orchestrating a lifestyle that will benefit both of them and their children immeasurably. Every woman interviewed in this group used the word "partner" or "equal" to describe her relationship with her husband. They both know that it takes their combined efforts to make success happen. Loretta, who is the wife of a wealthy corporate executive, admitted honestly, "He wouldn't have any of this if it weren't for me."

When Janice and Bill married, she stopped work as soon as her two sons were born and has never been interested in a full-time career since. Her life is busy and full and she puts in quite a long day making sure that everything goes smoothly for the family. Bill remarks often how much he appreciates her taking care of everything so that he can focus on his work. He once told her, "As stressful as my job is, there would be no way I would get very far for us if you weren't handling the home front. If you had a career, especially one with any pressure and were as stressed as I am from a job of your own, I couldn't stand it."

The men who are married to these women appreciate and love them immensely for "holding down the fort." They respect their considerable skills and know it's not easy raising their children and managing the expensive homes and lifestyles they have made possible through long hours at the office. The "new and improved" cheerleaders are not just housewives, especially the television housewives that the baby boomers watched on "I Love Lucy" and "The Donna Reed Show." The days are now busier and more complicated than they were for Lucy, whose biggest challenge was to figure out how she and Ethel could get into Ricky's show.

These women are no less capable than their husbands but have opted for the traditional roles in our society, fitting any desires they have for a career of their own around that priority. They have, in effect, contributed their personal resources to the good of the unit. In many cases, the effect of these "partnerships" has been secure families with money. They are among the most privileged in our society, but handling all that comes with being privileged requires women who are not only energetic but also savvy.

Several of the women in this group said that their mothers who did not work out of the home were their role models. They were the classic cheerleaders of the past many of whom, unlike their baby boom daughters, had no college education. But they were smart, charming and clever in juggling their lives, managing the sometimes meager resources. They were also cheerful and pleasant women who rarely complained, at least not outwardly, exhibiting a "joie de vivre" that their daughters in this study wanted to emulate. They were on the go, and in addition to raising their children and having the father's slippers ready at the door, these mothers also added to their days volunteering in the community and at church. Busy as it was at times, life was simpler then and, like the cheerleaders in the sixties, the routines were often less complex than today's in many ways.

Selfish Selflessness

One cheerleader who is the wife of a wealthy businessman said she "worked very hard in order to keep herself looking good for her husband and the role she has to play." In addition to taking charge of rearing her children, she takes excellent care of herself, spending hours a week at the health club with a trainer and keeping bi-weekly appointments with the hairdresser and manicurist. She works on perfecting her entertaining, keeping track of their social engagements on a master calendar in her study and taking care to maintain their social contacts. She constantly updates her wardrobe and the stays abreast of current trends in home decorating. She is an active member of several civic organizations, especially the garden club. She is well liked and respected as a prominent citizen in her community. Clearly, she has a full-time job. To most women not so fortunate financially, this "job" sounds like luxury but she doesn't see it that way. Doing all of these things simply helps her be the best she can be and it helps not just her, but her husband as well. There are definite arenas in which one is trained for this job. Cheerleaders go to camp; baby boom cheerleaders go to committee meetings.

Some of these women are tormented by wanting to have it all—career and family—and all of the advantages that come with both. One woman gave up the career she loved to have a family, but later had second thoughts about whether she was depriving herself of something she really wanted to do. "One of the hardest things I have to struggle with is my desire still to have some kind of professional identity and yet do everything that I think needs to be done for my family. I don't want to give up the flexibility I need so I made the decision to give up a career. Frankly, I'm not sure I want to work that hard. Why wear myself out doing both and risk not enjoying either. Most days I'm not sorry I made the decision I did. But I do wonder from time to time if I somehow should have tried harder to manage to do both."

Smile—Win or Lose

Accomplished cheerleaders learn early that one of their most important jobs is to be upbeat and positive whether the team is winning or not. After all, bad behavior or poor sportsmanship from the sidelines reflects poorly on the school or the team. Women in this group said that this is also true for them as they serve as the cheerleaders for their husbands and children.

Ruth described an incident when she didn't keep this in mind. Her daughter was highly ranked in the state as a cross-country runner and Ruth never missed the opportunity to cheer for her at meets. One day, after her daughter whizzed by, she saw another runner who was obviously struggling with a stitch in her side. Instead of cheering for this opponent or saying nothing, she yelled "Slow down!" Not being an athlete herself, she thought it made sense to give into the pain. Surely no one heard her or would mind if they did. But much to her embarrassment, another mother shot a surprised and disapproving glance her way and her husband glared at her. Lesson learned: No matter how partisan a cheerleader you are for your team, always be a good sport.

One of the skills most professional wives master early to be successful is the fine art of "working a room" at a social function. One of the women in the study described how she studied the effective way her husband's boss and wife always graciously entered the room, separated into different areas and made sure everyone was spoken to before the evening was ended. "They were so warm and made everyone feel comfortable and at home. They immediately became my role models."

It's not always easy for cheerleaders to smile in the faces of those who have hurt their loved ones. Gloria has been a minister's wife for many years and still finds it difficult to keep her mouth shut when members of the congregation, no matter how well meaning they might be, say something about her husband or how he is doing his job. It is especially hard when she knows the details about a situation and, out of respect for her husband's position, cannot say a word.

Advice, not Criticism

Stacy is the wife of John, a high-level university administrator. By definition, people in such positions live in a world where they receive daily, sometimes hourly criticism. Even the thickest of skins grows weary of constant second-guessing and offers of a better way to do things. A man in such a position is always aware of the fact that the people who are so quick to judge usually have an agenda of their own and a self-serving reason to make certain suggestions. At the end of the day, he comes home tired and battle weary.

At the end of some days, however, John wants to share the headaches with Stacy, someone in whom he has confidence and with whom he can vent frustrations in safety. Since she has been trained as a counselor and is somewhat objective, her insights and suggestions are invaluable to him. Once, soon after John had been promoted to this position, he told her about a difficult incident and how he handled it. Stacy immediately suggested a better way to do it, thinking of course that he'd like honest feedback. Wrong! To John, it felt like unwelcome criticism. They decided that in the future, he would tell her up front whether he needed "honest feedback" (a euphemism for criticism) or just a sounding board.

Sometimes, husbands don't want advice at all. Once, Claire tried very hard to influence Phil's decision about whether to fire a woman in the company who had been sleeping with several of the higher level partners. The affairs had destroyed three marriages and all three of the wives were close friends of Claire. The situation was complicated and Phil tried to explain that there were many reasons he couldn't take her advice, reasons he could not discuss with her. Claire saw him as weak and realized as the months passed that her attitude was affecting their own marriage. The issue wasn't worth that, so she backed off, vowing not to become involved again.

The cheerleaders of the 1950's and 1960's were ornaments rather than partners on the team. The husbands of baby boom cheerleaders usually want and value advice from their wives. In fact, many readily admit that they almost always make better decisions when they listen. After all, she has only one motive— helping the home team win. Not being in the direct line of fire also means that cheerleaders are sometimes in a position to hear things from the sidelines that can even help the team do the right thing. Gloria once overheard several of the church members whispering during a service about how long and boring some of her husband's sermons had been lately. She told him about it that night and he worked harder to "spice up the message" for the next Sunday.

Gloria's husband listens when she speaks. Another time, they were invited to a dinner party at the home of a prominent church member. Her husband suggested they take a bottle of wine but Claire felt that the hosts might be offended. He was sure it would be fine but by the time they arrived at the house, she had convinced him to leave the wine in the car. As they entered, the hostess said, "Let me get you some apple cider. We hope you like that. We don't drink and don't associate with those who do.

Public/Private People

Most women in this group have husbands who are high profile. Living in a fishbowl is hard on families, especially children. It usually falls to the cheerleader to make sure all the children have enough room to grow and live as freely as possible without the unnecessary pressure of people judging their every move. Just look at the fiercely protective behavior of Hillary Clinton where Chelsea is concerned.

As a military wife, Paula knew all too well how costly missteps of the children or herself could be to Frank's career. With Frank being a high-ranking officer in a visible position, everyone constantly watched what they did. Paula recalls that when they first drove onto the base after they were married, Frank, who is usually easy going and relaxed, pointed to a speed limit sign and said emphatically, "You will not ever speed on this base!" Paula took her role seriously, working hard never to do anything that might embarrass Frank. She did the same where the children were concerned. When they were stationed in

Germany, she reminded them frequently that they were to behave well at all times. "You are first and foremost American citizens and children of an Army officer," she said. "It is a privilege for you to be here."

Competing Through the Team— Not With the Team

As Paula knew all too well, there is perhaps no more competitive organization than the military. Promotions and perks are all based on rank and the rank of one's husband determines in effect the status of his wife. How the wife plays her part is critical. In fact, military men are still informally rated on their wives. It was not unusual for women who were not appropriately involved in the activities on base to be dismissed by other wives for "not being team players." Frank is Paula's second husband and they married at a point in Frank's career when he held the rank of lieutenant colonel. The wife of a major once remarked to Paula, "You're certainly marrying at the right level, dear." Paula, who had climbed the military ladder as an Army nurse, replied, "True, I was never married to a lieutenant or captain. I was one."

Being able to hold one's own is a requirement of the professional wife if she is going to help her husband do what he wants to do. She must negotiate a world within a world. Somehow she must strike the delicate balance between supporting her husband by getting along with the other wives and not overshadowing her husband in any way.

The standings of teams in most athletic competition are a reflection of whose team is doing better. If your football team goes into postseason competition, then you go into postseason play. If yours is the last-ranked basketball team in the conference, then you are a low-ranking player. For many women in this group, this principle also holds true.

The Wind Beneath Their Wings

Of all the sports, the cheerleading season is the longest. It lasts all year and requires that participants not only commit their time and energy to attending the games and practices, but to do this for all of the sports, several of which are going on at the same time. In any fall college season, cheerleaders are supporting soccer, hockey, football and basketball, and often two or more sports events in one day. The life of the baby boom cheerleader is just as packed. There are great expectations from her husband and children that everything will be done well and on time—and it invariably is. They know she will always show up for the game, no matter what the game is, and that she will always be cheering for them. She is the proverbial "wind beneath their wings" and they appreciate how important she is to everything they do. Her enthusiasm and devotion to the 'team" is the key. She'll create a beautiful environment for holidays and special occasions, remember everyone's favorite meal and charm sophisticated dinner guests with her wit and intelligence. Shelia said, "Last Christmas after dinner, I stood in the doorway of my kitchen and watched everyone laughing and talking in our living room. This is what I love the most and I am proud that I made that happen." In the minds of their families, baby boom cheerleaders make everything happen.

Chapter 5

THE BASEBALL PLAYER

"Safe at Home"

W_{HEN} Elizabeth was in the first grade in the early 1950's, she spent some of every afternoon playing "teacher" with her dolls. She gave her Ginny doll A's and reprimanded Howdy Doody for not sitting up straight. Sometimes he would have to miss recess. She loved to write on her small chalkboard and have "lessons" for her students. Elizabeth's mother was a teacher in the same school and it was always a special treat for Elizabeth to putter in her classroom as she waited to go home, writing on the real chalkboard and dusting erasers. She was in her element. Even at six years old, she knew that she wanted to be a teacher like mom.

Teaching was one of the most respected careers to which a woman could aspire in the 1950's. Like nursing and social work, the profession represented the best of all worlds for women at that time. They could be educated (but not too much), make money (but not too much), and still be able to indulge their natural, feminine predispositions for nurturing and caring for others. If they married, they could have convenient hours that allowed them to have a career and still be home with their families in the afternoons, evenings and summers. Role models reinforced these notions for women, such as the familiar television personality of the 1950's, "Our Miss Brooks," as they pursued this calling with the blessings of our society.

Home and traditional occupations, such as teaching, nursing, and social work, have provided channels of creative expression for many baby boom women. These women have combined traditional roles with their personal aspirations in a way that has led to satisfying and productive lives. Professions that value teamwork and the desire to make the world a better place attract women who are like baseball players. Building on time-honored American values rooted in our Constitution, they work to "promote the general welfare" of their communities and "insure domestic tranquility" for their families. To accomplish this, they seek familiar and accepted ways to meet this goal.

Intricate Simplicity

Elizabeth and her approach to life can readily be compared to that of a baseball player. Americans love baseball and accept it as a pleasant athletic pastime, one that is easily understood and relaxing to watch. On the surface, the rules of the game appear simple enough and the pace lets you leisurely enjoy hotdogs and sing "Take Me Out to the Ballgame." Baseball is one team sport that most people have actually played at some time and it remains the only major sport many can actually picture themselves playing throughout much of their lives if they want to. Professional baseball players are certainly physically fit enough to play the sport and can endure games that last for hours. But they don't seem to have the bodies and physical stature required of some other, more demanding, sports. They are therefore less imposing and thus less threatening. Two of the best examples are Pete Rose, who's been described as too short, too old and too slow and Babe Ruth who was even a glutton and a heavy drinker. But they became two of baseball's greatest players. These athletes seem more like us—average

Americans out for a fun afternoon. Naturally, we like them. We're drawn to them and have been so since the 1880's. It's not called the "American pastime" for nothing.

However, any true fan who has spent many hours observing baseball knows that it isn't as simple as it might appear. There are intricacies in executing plays that make or break a team. Sportswriter Phil Hersh's description of a play that only took an instant is typical of the game:

> The batter hit a ground ball that looked like a live grenade, but the shortstop fielded it and threw it to the second baseman. As the second baseman crossed second, he was upended by the runner moving from first base to second. whose clean, hard slide drove the second baseman's throw to be off-line. The first baseman instantly moved in the throw's direction, grabbed it and reached back to tag the batter out. Double play. End of inning.

The illusion of simplicity is one of the reasons Americans like the sport so much. It doesn't seem like rocket science to them. Watching a game also doesn't mean that they will be sitting on the edge of their seats with heart-stopping anticipation for several hours as in many other sports. According to Carlton Fisk, the Hall of Fame White Sox catcher, "Any schnook can play it, and they do play it, at all levels, whether it is stickball in the streets or rockball in the country." Yet, in fact, it is extremely complicated.

Social work, nursing and teaching are somewhat the same way. We think we understand these "simple" occupations. For example, all of us have been required by law to be exposed to teachers to observe them and what they do. It looks understandable enough. Therefore most people become self-styled experts on these three professions and will readily tell anyone how each should be done. Without hesitation, people advise nurses and social workers on how they should treat their patients and clients and they tell teachers how they should teach our children. For women in these fields, unlike other professions, society has historically defined even their character and their appearance. Like baseball, people love to umpire from the sidelines. But it is only those who truly comprehend the sport who really know how complex each play is.

Whenever people think they understand fully what others are doing, whether it is a sport or a profession, they tend to have one of two attitudes. They may de-value the profession and people who participate in it, feeling that "anyone can do it." This makes teachers, social workers and nurses feel a lack of respect for the work they do. Low wages and minimal benefits reinforce this attitude.

Even rookies can become deluded by the stereotype. For example, Kelly, a teacher for twenty-five years, recalls a conversation with June, a new student teacher preparing her first lesson for a middle school science class. June told her that she had worked hard on the lesson and knew a lot about this topic. It was "a piece of cake," she said. "After all, how hard could it be?" Kelly looked at the June's lesson plan and pointed out flaws. She also told her that what she had prepared would probably take only 15 minutes, even though the class lasted 55 minutes. When June insisted she could make the lesson work well, Kelly decided to let her learn the hard way. The class began and the students immediately began to flood her with questions about what they should do. Some began to jump ahead to work on parts of the lesson that hadn't been explained, others lost interest and misbehaved. In exactly fourteen minutes, the lesson she had prepared was finished. June looked desperately at Kelly for help. She'd just gained a new respect for teaching.

On the other hand, some people tend to sit on the sidelines in awe of these workers, amazed at what they can do. Parents cover teachers' desks at the end of the year with gifts and notes of appreciation for "miracles" teachers have performed with their children. Likewise, women in these professions often hear years later from students they've taught or from patients or clients they've helped who tell them how their work touched their lives. Mary saves every note and gift that students have sent her. She calls them her "trophy case." For every student who actually thanked her, she hopes there are many others who feel the same way.

Our society is ambivalent about these professions just as it is about the sport of baseball. We balk at the notion of paying teachers or nurses more money and even tell our most promising children that while we want them to have good teachers, we don't want them to become teachers. We want them to be doctors—anyone can be a nurse. Bobbie has supervised the training of nurses for years and says that one of the saddest things she hears from her students is that they believe the message of their parents and society. "They have come to think that they are simply not smart enough to be doctors, even though some say that becoming a physician would have been their preference."

Even though we patiently endure the petulant demands of athletes in other sports when they insist on astronomical salaries, we as a nation have been less tolerant of baseball strikes. Likewise, when teachers strike, people often say how wrong it is for them to deprive the children of their education. Nurses and social workers also are underpaid. But it doesn't trouble the nation enough to raise their salaries. After all, aren't they missionaries who are answering a "calling?" What right do they have want more money like other professionals?

As American as Apple Pie

All baseball players are not alike. In the extreme, some of these women may feel "less than" in many ways. They think that their work is taken for granted and dismissed by those with more money or power. Over time, they may even begin to wonder if it isn't true. Maybe their work isn't important. Maybe they aren't important. This can lead to low self-esteem in the women and ultimately hurts the professions they represent. On the other hand, boomer baseball players may feel that their role is crucial for society and are ready to fight to make the perception of their careers better. They are vocal advocates for their fields. They also may be know-it-alls. For example, we have all encountered the teacher who corrects people's grammar or the nurse who doesn't hesitate to dole out medical advice. Clearly, of course, most boomer women who are baseball players fall somewhere in the middle of these two extremes.

These women are generally comfortable conforming to the expectations and rules of society. They try to please the powers that be. Teaching, nursing and social work are traditional fields; baseball is a traditional sport. There is safety and security in following the expected patterns, ones that allow our women "baseball players" to choose these careers. They can simultaneously thrive as the keepers of their households and the nurturers of the next generation and those in need. Likewise, baseball is an accepted and approved game. Even the terminology of baseball includes such nice terms as "safe" and "home base." Other sports end in "sudden death" whereas baseball goes into "extra innings." Their players make "errors," which are, after all, perfectly human and understandable. The women we interviewed who had children put family above work, although at given times during their lives they pursued both goals. Those without children said that family and work were equally important to them. Interestingly, all of the boomer baseball players we interviewed were married. No other group we describe in this book have just one marital status represented.

Simple Equals Happy

These women are simple and clear about the purpose of their lives. They thrive in their domesticity and the predictability of their routines. They are happy and content with what they do. They are positive and fulfilled women who experience a congruence in their daily work and in their role within their homes. They have senses of humor and laugh at the some of the antics of their students and patients and situations at work. They look on the bright side. Yes, they feel overwhelmed and stressed at times with their many responsibilities or when things go wrong. But by temperament and through experience, they have developed a workable mechanism for keeping themselves productive and happy despite problems.

Mary remembers many times in her thirty years as a teacher when the sheer love for the students and her desire to help them kept her from quitting. "In one situation, I had to teach in a mobile unit with over forty students each period of the day. Many of the students were troubled teen-agers who lived in a poor, rural community. Their parents were suspicious of the school officials and teachers, were wary of 'too much book learnin,' and questioned everything from the credentials of the teachers to the textbooks used. 'I don't want my kids being taught by some northerner who don't understand how we do things here,' they would say. In many meetings with parents, she was told more than once that "they would have her job if she didn't start assigning the books they wanted the students to read." She explained that she was following the state-approved curriculum but this didn't satisfy them. To make matters worse, she and the other teachers in her school were rarely supported by the school administration where discipline was concerned. If students decided they didn't like a teacher, they would kill a small animal and cover the teacher's car with its blood or put garbage on her desk before she arrived at school. Mary describes the two years she spent there as "the biggest test of my desire to teach at all costs."

These are women most people would describe as "nice" and while they have pride in themselves and what they do, they aren't generally egotistical. Not usually self-conscious or uncomfortable with people, they are also are among the stable elements of most communities. They are dependable. In many ways, they are the glue of society as well as of their homes. They understand themselves and the unique gifts they have to contribute. They don't seek situations in life that are defined by high pressure. They just want to be a valued part of their neighborhoods, to have a niche on a team that aims for the good of everyone. They want to fit in and play a useful role. It is a simple plan they have created for their lives and it works.

Team Camaraderie but Alone When at Bat

Teachers, nurses and social workers function well with other teachers in settings that, by definition, offer opportunities for support and shared concerns with fellow workers. They are a team, in effect, operating in tandem with others who have a common mission of serving children, patients or clients. They share materials, stories about their students and patients and cover each other's classes or shifts when the need arises. As in baseball, there is a regular use of substitutes and "pitch hitters." These women are remarkably flexible when it comes to doing what needs to be done, usually without ever questioning why. They celebrate each other's birthdays and invest in each other's lives outside of school. In school, one often finds the teachers' lounges stocked with donuts and homemade goodies. In short, these women take care of each other much like they take care of everyone in their lives.

A psychiatric nurse, Bobbie, describes the dependence on teammates. Teamwork is not only a matter of using the expertise of the other nurses, but more significantly, it is a matter of safety. "When your clients are volatile, unstable and sometimes violent people, everyone must watch out for everyone else," she explains. If you turn your back, you must be able to depend on the others to cover you if a patient attacks." They also learn in their training to be able to identify quickly each other's strengths and weaknesses. "It is impossible to know everything. So if we are not totally comfortable in a certain area, without hesitation, we will pass it on to another nurse. The job we have to do is more important than our ego."

These women are "belongers." One of the best parts of the career choices they make is being part of a group. They accept and like others. In return, they want to be accepted and liked as well. Kelly, a teacher, says that one of the best parts of her day is when she has the opportunity to meet with the others on her "team." They are able to share ideas, determine the best possible way to work with a difficult student, and listen to each other's concerns and frustrations. "Much of our strength and overall effectiveness is in our ability to function well as a unit," she says.

Likewise, baseball players know that while they may sit in the dugout together waiting for their turn at bat, they each will be at the plate alone trying to get a hit for the team. The quality of the work these women do, whether in a classroom or with each patient or client, depends on their unique skills and their ability to handle each situation by themselves. When the bell rings, teachers will close the door and face the classroom alone. Keeping her eye on the ball, a teacher will ignore the squirming of other students and annoying blasts from the intercom as she helps Sue with a math problem. A nurse will ignore the demands of the patient who wants a blanket as she attempts to stop the bleeding of a head wound. A social worker tries to avoid being distracted by the ringing phone and the rising stack of caseloads on her desk as she discusses one situation with a court counselor. These women make numerous complex and important decisions all day—and they make it look easy. They are alone but not alone. They are all secure in the knowledge that they can get help from others on the team if it is needed, just as the baseball player knows that, even if he only hits a single, another teammate will step up to the plate to drive him home.

Long Season/Progress Can Be Slow

Baseball is a long, slow game. It can last for hours and to the casual observer, it may seem like an eternity before the action gets exciting or the score changes. Likewise, teaching and nursing have long seasons. Progress in children comes slowly and while there are periodic flashes of excitement when "the light bulb comes on," it can feel like the movement of a glacier. Nurses and social workers patiently wait for improvement in many of their seriously ill patients or deeply troubled clients. It's a daily reality of the job.

These women go into their professions aware that they are facing nine long innings and perhaps extra innings. They are mentally and emotionally prepared for what they face and know that they have to make each inning—especially the one they're in at the moment—as successful as possible. True, some find the slow process too difficult to endure and they leave. But the ones who stay are inspired by the desire to make a difference with children or the people with whom they work. Lorraine remembers being a freshman in college and not being sure what to major in. She considered nursing as only one of many possibilities. One day, she was assisting in the university hospital and was asked to wash the feet of an indigent, diabetic woman who clearly had not bathed in some time. She remembers how repulsive the task was until she looked into the eyes of the patient who was smiling at her. "There was such gratitude and appreciation for what I was doing that I began to feel genuine joy in making her more comfortable," Lorraine recalls. I saw the value of what even a small gesture like this could do for people and from that moment on, I knew nursing would be my profession."

Big Fishes in Small Ponds

Teachers have center stage as they control classrooms. They determine the environment, the pace and the nature of each day's lessons and decide what constitutes fairness for their students. It's their world, and they have power over what happens, at least while the door is closed. One teacher said, "I love the work and literally bask in the richness of the classroom environment. It transcends the school and I try to ignore the hassles outside my door. The magic of the kids sustains me."

But ignoring the hassles outside her door isn't always easy to do. The worlds they control are within walls of much larger schools and while they have autonomy in their own room, they have almost none in the larger context. Their profession is influenced and ultimately controlled by school boards, and parents, legislators, and administrators. And sometimes when the teacher's goals clash with those who make the rules, these well-intentioned women suffer unbearable stress. "It is not unusual to receive a directive from central administration that requires us to change what we are doing immediately," says Gloria, an elementary principal. "Not only were we not involved in the decision, we are not given much real opportunity to argue against it or to request more time to implement the changes smoothly. And if it doesn't work well, we will be blamed."

At home, almost all of the women in this type said they are either in charge or share control of the home front with their husbands—and they like it that way. In many cases, they manage the money as well. They like making their corner of the world, even if small, a haven of order and organization. Elizabeth said, "I have no desire to get a bigger job. My husband makes more money than I do and his job determines the overall direction of our lives in many ways. But I run the show in my classroom and at home, and this arrangement is fine for us."

Boomers who are baseball players want to be the best that they can be at whatever they do. They're willing to spend long hours and work hard to perfect their game. Most of the teachers and nurses in our study had masters degrees and had won awards or been recognized in some way for their accomplishments. Sometimes the rewards are more personal and less visible to others. Victoria said that while she has had many "highs" as a teacher, she cherishes most the memory of an older man she taught to read. He credited her with being one of the people who had most changed his life.

Closet Confidence

These women give incredible energy to professions that can provide them with tremendous satisfaction. As they grew up, it was not unusual to hear of teachers working in classrooms for 40 years. But times have changed and the expectations of society for these individuals have gradually become quite overwhelming. On many days, the profession extracts more of teachers than it gives. Miss Crump in the 1960's had the luxury of focusing all of her attention on the geography or spelling lesson for the day. Today's teachers face more complicated issues like the curriculum and mammoth social problems children bring to schools. Not only do they have to solve every child's social or emotional problem, society expects teachers to deliver higher test scores and be more and more accountable.

With all these headaches, how do the women in these professions keep up their self-esteem? Surprisingly, our boomer baseball players are confident and secure people who feel good about themselves and their achievements. They are sure about their abilities and skills to do their jobs. They know they are good at what they do and are now leaders in their fields. One social worker said that there is a sense of power that comes when you know that you go where no one else is willing to go: "I do that every day when I try to save a family from self-destruction in parts of the city that should be condemned as unsafe for anyone." Likewise, a nurse said she feels "noble" in her commitment to her patients. "There is often no internal support for you as you work but I think that I am good enough to overcome that. What I do is important."

Satisfaction

At fifty, however, these noble women are also tired. They're tired of the toll taken by the daily battles. They're tired of the increasing pressure to work with more and more troubled people, tired of responding to a more demanding public. Many plan to leave their professions as soon as they can get retirement benefits. One nurse said she is leaving because the personal caregiving that attracted her to the profession in the first place is less than it was when she began. "Nurses have lost much of their autonomy in terms of how they are able to give patients what we think they need. HMO's are forcing doctors to send them home sooner and we have less contact with them. The essence of care now is technology."

While many women in this type are ready to leave the field as soon as they can, they have no regrets about the choices they have made so far in their lives. They still love and respect their professions. Many will continue to volunteer at hospitals, schools and agencies for years to come. They find tremendous satisfaction in the memories of the people they have helped, in the friendships they have formed with colleagues. The "highs" have far outweighed the "lows" and their lifestyle has been exactly what they envisioned. Almost without exception, the dreams and type of life they said they wanted for themselves when they were in college came true. At fifty, they say that they are content and have been so through the years. Theirs was a career played for the love of the game. They have worked hard to help the helpless and keep the world from falling apart for countless people. The best part was that they could do all of that and still be home in time to fix dinner.

Chapter 6

THE LAP SWIMMER

"The Horizontal Climb"

Six a.m. The alarm signals the start of a new day. Today, tomorrow, the day after . . . each day is remarkably similar to the day before. The routine is set. A healthy breakfast, a quick look at the newspaper, then on to the pool to join the Master Swimmers. Once there Joan pulls on a swimsuit much like the suit of every other swimmer. She covers her waist length hair with a swim cap, keeping it out of her face, eyes and mouth as she swims. With no hesitation, Joan plunges into the cold water. Lap after lap, she swims up and down the pool, and up and down the pool again.

Joan is joined by other swimmers just as passionate about their sport. Each of them is careful to stay in her own lane, following the etiquette of the pool, obeying the rules. They are undisturbed by swimmers on either side of them. At times the swimmers vary their stroke from the crawl to the butterfly or the breaststroke, but the rhythm and grace of the swim are constant. While they are swimming it is hard to tell one swimmer from the next.

Joan decides before she begins exactly how long she will swim. At the end of her workout, she hurries to the locker room, sheds her bathing suit, and changes into her street clothes to begin her workday. She feels refreshed, competent, proud of the discipline she has demonstrated in getting up at the break of day and going to the pool to exercise.

The payoff from such a disciplined sport is not so obvious to those who see Joan's car in the parking lot day after day after day. To the casual observer it seems boring and repetitive. Dragging yourself out of bed at the break of day, fitting into a nondescript, unrevealing bathing suit, and doing the same thing over and over again, holds no appeal for many. Joan knows that none of this is true. She engages in one of the most popular sports in America. Her sport has stood the test of time, and to those willing to commit, it promises good health, a streamlined body, and a tranquil soul.

Master Swimmers

Master swimming, a nationwide competitive swimming program for adults, promotes physical fitness through training and competitive swimming. Competition within five-year age groups attracts swimmers from as young as twenty-five to as old as ninety-five, and older. Swimming pools across the country support this program by letting adult swimmers practice daily for competition and health. Day after day they arrive in the early hours of the morning or the late hours of the evening, after other swimmers have left, to practice and prepare. This is a sport lacking in glamour and publicity. But the faithful enjoy its recreational, social, emotional, and physical rewards.

The women we call lap swimmers have professional lives that mirror that of the lap swimmer who perseveres to become a master. They commit to a course in their professional life that is quiet, repetitive, routine. They dive into a pool and, once there, they stay the course. Day after day, week after week, month after month, year after year, they return to their place of work to keep their head down, focus on their job, and hope that when their time comes they will have joined the ranks of the masters.

Paula is one of our master swimmers. After college, she took the civil service exam and placed high enough to get an attractive job with the government. For twenty years, she has worked in the same office with the same people, taking only a few years off to start her family. She has a better-than-average salary, excellent benefits, and the security of knowing she has a job she can do. At one point, her husband thought his corporation was going to relocate him. Paula researched the options available for her and found a job similar to the one she was doing. She was thrilled. She could move, do essentially the same work, and because it was also with the government, lose none of her benefits. "Can you believe it?" she exulted. "The same job, salary, hours. It's perfect." She had security no matter where she was. She could swim in another pool with the same benefits of her present one.

Our Master Swimmers have paid the price to become good at what they do. They work for years at the same job perfecting their strokes. Now they are content in a job that is comfortable and not demanding. They pride themselves on their accomplishment. They like having a secure niche. "I can't imagine wanting to be anywhere else," admits one.

The Rules of the Pool

Lap swimmers are limited to when and where they can swim. Once they get to the pool, they accept the importance of following the rules of that pool. "No swimming after 10 p.m." "Children not allowed to swim without an adult." "Stay in your lane." "Allow faster swimmers to pass." Our swimmers also learn the rules of the career game they choose. Policies and procedures, bound in thick manuals, guide every step. Rather than finding this constraining, swimmers find it liberating. Not having to worry about the unpredictable allows them to expend all their energy accomplishing the job at hand.

Carla works in a library. She loves the structure and order of her work. "I feel so at home among the rows and rows of books, each carefully categorized and put on the proper shelf," she explains. "All I have to do is make sure everything is done. I don't even have to decide how to do it!" She embraces the library rules, glad to enforce them if a visitor steps out of line. Carla is a lap swimmer. A happy one at that.

Four Strokes: One Lane

Swimmers rely on four basic strokes: the crawl, the breaststroke, the backstroke, and the butterfly. In competition, they usually swim one stroke during an event, but in practice they freely swim the strokes in any combination. In fact, these combinations help prevent boredom. The swimmers in our study have roles they can play in their workplace. Many of them have spent at least some time in administrative positions as well as in the work most identified with their organization, such as teaching, therapy, or computer analysis. But the nature of the roles is limited. For example, the hats worn by Molly, a professor we interviewed, vary somewhat as she is teacher, mentor, consultant, and contributor, but her basic daily routine never changes. Often the life of this professor seems solitary, uneventful. Writing and lecturing require extended time for preparation. At times she may seem limited. She doesn't know or even want to know much about those disciplines she has not chosen to pursue. Her passion is for her field. She stays in her lane.

Tread Water or Float

Learning to tread water and to float are valuable to the swimmer. If she becomes tired or cramped, she can rest by floating or simply treading water. She can do it for a long time. The water's buoyancy gradually and gently relaxes the swimmer. It is almost like a return to the mother's womb. Experience teaches the swimmers that even when they are at their worst, the water in the pool will support them. If they have a heart attack, or sprain an ankle, or if they are depressed, overweight, whatever their problems great or small, the water will surround them and they will be soothed. It's no secret that swimming is often prescribed by doctors as part of the healing ritual for many ills.

Ideally, the "pool" of the boomer lap swimmers also supports them. It provides financial, emotional, and social security. Raises are given yearly. No one is likely to be fired or even laid off. In some cases there is even a protection against the administrators deciding that someone should be fired. For example, in a college setting Molly has tenure and cannot lose her job except in extreme cases. She has job security not found in most settings. In the face of illness there is unlikely to be criticism, only concern and support, often to the point of others doing the job for the individual. Such work settings are rare. Government positions offer much the same security. Once the probation time is past, it is very difficult to fire someone. If an individual stays for the required number of years with the government, she too will be rewarded with ongoing benefits. At retirement, she will continue to receive income almost as high as when she was working and will be eligible for health insurance for the rest of her life.

Lynn was a government employee. She had been on the job for a short period of time when her son was involved in a serious car accident. She had to spend many hours, sometimes days, away from work to care for him. The rest of the organization chipped in their sick days so that she would not lose pay while she was out with her son. The staff also divided up her work when she was gone so that when she returned she would not suffer the problems of being so far behind. The "pool" supported her. The organization made it possible for co-workers to help by allowing one employee to transfer sick days to another. After such support from her work family, it would be hard for Lynn to leave her job. As a single parent she recognizes the advantage of job security and organizational support.

Don't Splash

Swimmers don't like people who splash water on them when they are trying to swim. It throws off their concentration and destroys the tranquility of the water. It sometimes even chokes them. They also don't like swimmers to show up in inappropriate, sexy swimsuits. This is not a place to attract the opposite sex. When newcomers arrive they quickly learn it is not okay to dress seductively, distract others from their swim by being loud or boisterous, or attempt to talk to other swimmers while they are concentrating on their laps.

Our swimmers protect their work environment in the same way. If a newcomer enters the workplace and makes a "splash," she is likely to be met with icy stares, pursed lips, and cold shoulders. She must earn her position as "master swimmer." Only swimming, or in this case working for many hours, and thus earning the trust and respect of her colleagues will allow the newcomer to be accepted.

Tara worked in a department with all men. She was not one to flaunt her femininity, but she enjoyed being the only woman. The men sought her counsel for suggestions on how to care for their children, mend fences with wives, choose pictures or furniture for their offices. Tara was also an accomplished businesswoman. She was respected not only in her office but also in the national organization that supported her profession. Tara was happy and secure. That is, until Kate arrived on the scene. Kate was the same age as Tara, but without the professional reputation and experience. She was, however, a very likeable individual whom people enjoyed being around. Relationships in the office began to change. More often than not, the men began to seek out Kate for personal conversation, asking for her advice instead of Tara. Tara distanced herself from Kate. She never invited her to lunch or showed any inclination to be friendly toward Kate. Kate did not understand Tara's cold shoulder and was hurt by it. Finally Kate decided to leave. She refused to work in a place where she didn't feel welcomed, especially by the only other woman.

Never Vertical, Always Horizontal

In order to get anywhere, swimmers must remain horizontal. If they attempt to stand up they will interrupt their swim and the swim of anyone else who might be in their lane. Our swimmers don't stand up either—unless they are in shallow water. They go with the flow. They are amazingly loyal workers who support the higher ups of their organization. Consider Joan, a lieutenant in the army. She was told to discipline a member of her unit who didn't deserve the harsh punishment. At least not in Joan's mind. Despite her concerns, Joan did as she was told without question. "The chain of command must be respected," she explained. "If I start questioning my superiors it will only cause problems." The idea of challenging the boss is completely alien to Joan. For her, the Army's history of success in the past is enough to convince her of the wisdom of honoring protocol in the present.

The leadership in the workplace of the swimmers appreciates their support. Swimmers can always be counted on to follow orders. They willingly do the mundane tasks assigned them. If they want change, they request it with quiet and respectful dignity. The goals of the organization are important to them. They take care of the organization and the organization takes care of them.

But not always. Jane devoted her life to her job. She was a trainer for a large, well-respected organization that promoted a family atmosphere. Then the company was sold. The new buyer downsized. Jane had thought she would work there until retirement. Suddenly she was without a job, health benefits, and retirement income. Although the company offered to help her find a job, she took the plunge and started her own business.

"Being laid off was a real wakeup call," she realized. No longer would she trust any organization to take care of her.

Other swimmers wouldn't be chastened by Jane's experience. They feel they are safe in their organizations. If they keep their heads down and just keep doing what they are doing, they will be protected. Just as the water in the pool supports the swimmer, so too the work organization supports these women. Security and satisfaction await many swimmers. More often than not they are rewarded for their loyalty and longevity rather than their creativity. Like Mimi.

Mimi sat quietly in the auditorium. She had spent 25 years sitting in this same auditorium, attending these same types of presentations. But today was different. Today was her day. She was to be recognized in ways that she had dreamed of since the beginning of her career. Today the awards would be hers. Today she would find a measure of immortality in work. From now on an academic chair would bear her name. When first approached by the Dean, she modestly questioned the wisdom of choosing her to fill such an esteemed position. Her doubts were quickly appeased as her boss recounted the numerous contributions Mimi had made over the years. She had worked hard, done everything they had asked her to do, remained focused, and used all her energy to exceed the expectations she placed on herself as she worked hard to become the very best in her position. At last, she could claim her rightful place among other master swimmers.

Smooth Surface

Our lap swimmers, like the master swimmers, compete primarily with themselves. They have a vision of what they want to accomplish and work very hard to achieve their dreams. This work ethic does not go unnoticed by their superiors. They like structure and predictability. They may change "pools" just as a swimmer does not always swim in the same pool, but basically little changes. The talents and skills that allow them to be successful are the same, even if they change the setting in which they use them. Professional careers with the government, the military, education, and in some instances corporations attract the lap swimmer. Like Paula, the risks of change are minimized because the job is essentially the same, and where change is controlled, so too is stress.

Unfortunately the very same things that initially attracted the lap swimmer to the job can—in the worst-case scenario—over time disappoint them. Swimmers dive in thinking this is the greatest opportunity of their life, but after too many laps may find themselves unhappy and bored with jobs that are repetitive and unchallenging. Consider Connie.

Connie has been a teacher for over 20 years. She has lost the enthusiasm and energy she radiated at the beginning of her career. She went into teaching because she saw it as a mission. Too many changes in the definition of her role, too much paperwork, and a generation of children she doesn't understand leave her tired, frustrated, and angry. In the past year she has been to her physician four times complaining of back pain and fatigue. Her primary means of coping seems to come from the bottle of Zanex she religiously carries around in her pocketbook. An incident last year when she lost her temper with a student and spoke a little too harshly, and a lot too loudly, with language seen as unacceptable, scared Connie into seeking help. The real problem is that Connie is burned out. She has nothing left to give. "I have trouble dragging myself out of the bed in the morning. My only thought is how many hours before I can go home."

For her own good and that of her students, she needs to get out of the classroom altogether. Unfortunately, she is a single woman who can't afford to lose the income or the benefits of teaching another five years. So she stays, but she is "stuck." Listening to her talk, it is painfully clear that work is more like a jail sentence than the mission she so loved when she first entered the field, willing and eager to touch the hearts and minds of the children she taught.

All swimmers are not the same. They may look alike but under the surface some are satisfied and secure while others are disillusioned and stuck. Some swimmers swim for the joy of it, some because they feel they have to. Some swim to alleviate stress; others find the swim itself stressful. Some believe that they have to swim because giving it up might cause them problems while others, by swimming, are subjecting themselves to problems. Every day that they get up to go swim they hate it. But they do it anyway. Swimmers are like that. Some love their job, would do it anywhere, appreciate the repetition and the security of sameness. Others want to quit, but because of financial considerations can't. The work is the same, the quality of the work life, vastly different.

Go the Distance, But Not Too Far

Conditioned swimmers can swim miles before becoming winded. But no matter how far they swim, it is still within the confines of the pool. Our swimmers work hard year after year in the same job and they do seek and achieve promotions, better pay, and prestige. But they are limited. They can only go so far in their job before they hit the glass ceiling. The trade off for being in a highly structured job is giving up the freedom to go into uncharted waters. To stand in any one spot and see both ends, the middle, and the bottom of the pool is to agree to go no further. Lap swimmers don't swim in the ocean. They stay within the boundaries of the pool.

Their bosses define the job, direct the day, determine the pay, and decide on their promotions. Swimmers exchange freedom for security. The danger is this security becomes hypnotic. They become so relaxed they lose the ambition that might have characterized their early careers. One boomer was given the opportunity to write a book that would have made her a lot of money. Although she began the project with enthusiasm, the tedium of writing day after day when she didn't really have to drained her of her desire to continue the project.

"I had to give up too much," she said. "It wasn't worth it." Another described a lack of desire to learn new techniques on her job even though they were proven ways to accomplish her work faster and better. She had nothing to lose by not learning them. No one was going to make her learn and grow, so she didn't. "I've done okay this long, why change?" she admitted. Like her swimmer cohort, she valued her time and freedom more than being challenged by the possibility of becoming better, or the best, at what she did.

Whoever Leaves Last, Wins

Many sports are too strenuous for older athletes. Even swimming is harder and harder to do as each year passes. Getting up early, maintaining the discipline of practice, and traveling to competitions takes a strong commitment. But if they endure long enough, they are more likely to win competitions simply by virtue of the diminishing number of competitors. Their long-term commitment earns benefits and respect. They are allowed privileges not awarded to younger swimmers.

Seniority counts in the workplace of our swimmers. Some can and do swim for many years, even until they die. If they endure, they are honored and respected. In many settings even to be promoted the individual must remain with the organization for a specified period of time. An example would be a college campus where tenure and promotion are partly dependent on the number of years devoted to the institution. Our swimmers are in jobs they can keep for many years if their health holds up and if they wish to continue working. And these swimmers definitely wish to keep working. Most anticipate working until the organization requires them to quit. Their work is such an integral part of their identity that they cannot imagine life without it. Their senior status gives them privileges they value, such as prime office space, leadership of committees, representation at meetings, extended medical leave, longer vacation times, and a special role as a senior member of that academic institution, or mental health agency, or business corporation. They stay the course. They win the prize.

Big Pool, Little Swimmer

The water in the pool of the swimmer is constant. Swimmers come and go, but the water remains the same. So, too, in the organizations with our swimmers. They come and go, but the organization remains pretty much the same. With so many swimmers, each so much alike, any one swimmer is unlikely to be noticed as she leaves the pool. Kara worked for 10 years as head of her department. She brought it out of obscurity and chaos and into the spotlight as an exemplary program, recognized statewide for its excellence. Hour after hour, week after week, year after year, she devoted her time and energy to her job. When forced to leave for personal reasons, she slipped out of the water hardly noticed. A small party in her honor was attended by only a few of her fellow swimmers. Today almost no trace of her contributions is visible. "I gave that program my all, and what do I have to show for it? Nothing," she complains. "My colleagues didn't even bother to take twenty minutes of their time to wish me well." Kara left the pool prematurely, disillusioned and hurt. Another swimmer took her place. The swim continued.

Identical Start and Finish

Swimmers find the finish line of their swim to be very much like the starting line. One end of the pool is not much different from the other as long as you are swimming. Only time marks the boundaries from beginning to end, depending on how long the swimmer chooses to swim. Likewise, our swimmer's work at the beginning of her career is very similar to that at the close. She may swim with less effort, but she's still swimming.

Consider Joan, a social worker with a social service agency.

She started her career doing case management for clients. It was not a difficult job, but she found the contact with her clients highly rewarding. Her skill at her work and her leadership qualities led the director to promote her many times. Consequently she served in many roles, clinical and administrative, during her career. After more than 20 years of work, Joan was hungry for more time interacting with her clients. She was tired of any administrative duties and wanted to simplify her life. At her request she returned to her original role as a case manager. "This is why I got in this business in the first place," Joan stressed. Like Joan, the swimmer may spend time in other roles, such as administration. But often swimmers tire of the demands of complex duties and return to the original one that attracted them to the job in the first place. Remaining in the same situation over time, possibilities for change are limited. Just going through the paces feels sufficient.

Returning to her post as an English professor, Karen admitted, "I got tired of dealing with all the things that took me away from my first love, teaching. I couldn't be happier to be back in my office with my books and my students!" The importance of choice in the decisions of these women cannot be overstated. All decided they wanted to return to doing what they most loved about their job. They did not allow themselves to be stuck in roles that were not fulfilling personally and professionally. Or they changed jobs when necessary. Still the content of the job remained predictable.

The swimmer who is stuck is more likely to have had no choice in the first place or to have never varied the work that she has done. For example, Joyce was fascinated with computers. After college she took a job as a computer analyst with the government. The pay, the benefits, her coworkers, all made for a very attractive package. She was a good fit for their needs. Joyce worked for many years before she began to notice that she no longer looked forward to going to work. In fact she dreaded it. She began to miss more and more work as she seemed to come down with every virus, every cold, every infection anyone else had. At one point, she discovered she was likely to develop carpal tunnel syndrome if she didn't quit. But if she left, she jeopardized her retirement income, her health insurance, and her healthy income. If she stayed, she risked serious medical problems and burnout. Joyce was bored, depressed, disinterested, and dispirited. The job no longer "stroked" her, but she had done it so long and worked her way into such a narrow professional role that she had no good options for leaving. Or at least she felt this way. The repetition of the job became a physical and emotional drain, but Joyce felt stuck. So she was.

In It for Life

Swimming is a sport that many take up after trying other, more strenuous sports. Whether it is an injured knee, a weak back, a failing heart, athletes from other sports gravitate toward swimming. Weightlessness in the water is a welcome sensation, restoring health and the sense of well being. Some of our swimmers are those who have exhausted their energy on careers that have left them tired, worn down, and stressed out. They seek the structure and support of work settings such as government jobs or teaching institutions. Focusing on their work and not the peripheral demands of staff, billing, or insurance, is a welcome change from the stressful life they experienced in the private sector of business or the professions. They do not make as much money, but fewer working hours, more enjoyable working conditions, and less responsibility more than compensates for the loss. As one said, "Finally, I can enjoy being sick knowing I can stay home and read a book rather than pushing myself to go to work so I won't lose money."

These swimmers may have difficulty entering the ranks of the master swimmers. They start out elsewhere, so by definition they have to catch up with their co-workers. But they are happy to be part of an organization, not responsible for it. At the end of the day they can go home and forget work. They appreciate the newly found balance in their lives. Working, but not all the time, performing but not worrying. They have the confidence to believe they are valuable to the organization and will be able to work just as long as they wish. Having already gone through the stress of changing career direction, they are less likely to feel pressured by the fear of job loss. They feel secure, not stuck.

"Swimming is what you make it," proclaims the female swim guru, Jane Katz. How true for our swimmers as well. They can love or hate their job, make it challenging or reduce it to the ordinary, find ways to vary the routine or become so predictable they are hypnotized. For those who allow it to be routine and boring, the water is dangerous. But to those who make it all it can be, it is a solid job and a secure place in which to work, one that offers the flexibility to develop new talents and explore one's creativity.

Chapter 7

THE SAILOR

"Even Keel"

M ONDAY. Myra gives her secretary, Eileen, a copy of the agenda for the meeting. "Be sure to call everyone to find out what they want to drink with their meal," she tells her. "Oh, and order dinner for yourself as well. Even if you can't stay, I couldn't have done it without you!" Eileen beamed. Her boss's thoughtfulness was not unusual. No birthday, no holiday, no meeting, no completion of a project ever went by without Myra doing something to make Eileen feel she was important.

Tuesday morning. An important oversight committee is scheduled to review Myra's group. The visit is well-organized and professional. Myra has spent the night away from home to ensure that no distractions will prevent her from being sure everything is done and done well. Despite this important event, Myra doesn't forget Eileen. Just that morning she placed a beautiful plant on her desk with a note: "You're fantastic! How do you do it? Everything is perfect! Thanks so much for all you do to make us look good!"

Tuesday afternoon. Myra's bosses who will meet with the oversight committee have a detailed guide outlining what will be expected of them. Myra will not be satisfied with anything less than perfection. She wants the reviewers to go away thinking this is the best group they have seen. One last time she goes over every detail to be sure no one makes a mistake. Satisfied that everything is perfect, she trusts her team to do everything she has asked of them. She knows that their loyalty to her and their commitment to the job will guide them throughout the process.

Wednesday. The team visits and is impressed with a staff that obviously knows how to do its work exceptionally well. The supervisors articulate the philosophy of the organization with insight, integrity, and intensity, just as they have rehearsed so many times with Myra. They know the ropes, they can anticipate problems, and make adjustments when needed.

Thursday. The oversight committee congratulates all in Myra's group for their work. They have earned the highest of ratings. Myra is thrilled and can't say enough to thank her group and give them praise for all their preparation. Everyone involved feels that they have sailed through the process with amazing ease. Myra makes each participant believe that the success of the visit flowed from her participation.

Friday. Myra turns in her final report to the head of the company, citing the contributions of everyone involved, including Eileen. She writes notes to go in each person's file, documenting her importance to this crucial process.

At the end of the day Myra heads home, exhausted, but satisfied with her week's work.

Friday night. While Myra has been away her family has been well taken care of. She has left cooked meals in the refrigerator and encouraging notes on bathroom mirrors. She has assured each family member of her love and support. Myra hurries home, eager to turn her time and attention to her husband and children.

Saturday. Myra attends a track meet, entertains her husband's office staff for a holiday get together, and takes the evening meal over to her elderly parents. That night Myra's daughter makes the mistake of comparing Myra to her best friend's stay-at-home mom, complaining that Myra doesn't cook those good desserts like her friend's mom does. Myra loses it! She finds herself angry and resentful, lashing out at her daughter and reciting a litany of things she has done for her family. Much to her own and everyone else's surprise, she ends her tirade in tears, apologizing for becoming so upset over nothing.

*   *   *

Sailors! Anybody for a sail? Check the ropes, the rigging, the wind, the crew. Every detail must be attended to if the captain is to feel safe taking her boat out on the ocean. Myra is like a sailor. Her professional life as well as her personal life mirror a sailor's preparation. Sailing is a complex, complicated sport that requires elaborate preparation if a sail is to be successful.

Sailing can be done alone or with a crew. Alone, the skilled sailor pays close attention to all conditions important for the sport and ensures that all equipment is ready. By necessity, the boat is much smaller than one that requires a crew to sail. Many sailors prefer a larger boat and a crew whose members are trained or at least willing to follow the directions of the captain. If they know little themselves of what is required or why it is required, they put their trust in the captain, who instructs them in how they will play a part. Then all can share the experience of a relaxing, smooth experience.

Sailors may sail in different kinds of waters under varying conditions as well as in different sized sailboats. On the ocean, the sailor must understand the waves and the wind and use a compass when land is not in sight. On a lake, the challenge may be how to make the most of little wind or how to negotiate sailing while other watercraft create waves and threaten the serenity of the sail. Many accomplished sailors treasure the excitement and challenge of ocean sailing, while less experienced or more careful sailors prefer the safety of the lake where they can keep their destination in sight.

A long sail will leave the captain quite tired. It takes a lot of energy to concentrate on the mechanics of sailing, remain watchful for problems, direct the crew, and protect the boat from being unduly stressed by the conditions of the sail. Even so, when docking the boat the sailor must, in an equally careful manner, take down the sails, tie the ropes, store the sails, make sure the boat is covered appropriately, and see the crew safely on shore. The captain's job is not over until all details are complete and everyone else is off the boat. The captain will be the first one on and the last one off, taking responsibility both for the boat and for those with whom she sails.

Likewise, the sailors in our study are women who are ready and able to work alone or with other people. They assume responsibility for leading organizations or heading up projects. They help colleagues or friends reach their goals or help an organization accomplish its mission. They are willing to work with a variety of individuals, mentoring them, supporting them, or encouraging them. They tend to be in professional roles that lend themselves to these functions. For example, two of our sailors were heads of units within large organizations. Much of their work was administrative, but they also had a variety of other responsibilities where they worked along side their subordinates. Both said that the most rewarding part of their job was helping those with whom they worked to accomplish their goals.

In the extreme, sailors can be either catalysts on the one hand or enablers on the other. As catalysts, they are energetic, enthusiastic supporters who pull out all stops for people and projects with whom they are invested. Those who are the lucky beneficiaries of their involvement find that they are stimulated and inspired, knowing that the sailors have their best interest at heart. But all of these good intentions can still result in problems at times. In fact, some of the sailor's most impressive or endearing qualities can actually be the cause of some concern for her or her family. For example, sailors tend to be women who value both work and home. When they are able to balance this love of work and home, all is well. But when they attempt to be supermom and supercareer woman, they suffer.

Similarly, sailors appreciate the gifts of many other types of women and they can get into relationships that are more draining than they are rewarding. Some people and projects are better left alone. Thus, the boomer sailor may sometimes continue to invest time and resources into no-win situations. In these cases, there is a danger that people she is trying to help will become too dependent on her. The sailor enjoys doing things for other people, but, especially in these situations, she tends to exhaust herself. If she does not find ways to refuel after she empties herself in giving to her work, her family, and her friends, she can become tired, irritable, and depressed. She might help others remain dependent and irresponsible, rather than forcing them to be independent.

Myra is somewhere in the middle of these two extremes. She can be a great leader, capable of helping others reach their potential. But she can also overdo it at home and at work, leaving her little time for herself. Fortunately for sailors, their appreciation for other people makes them open to feedback from those they love and respect. These friends and family can tell them they are working too hard, taking their roles too seriously, or wearing themselves out. As Gloria says, "All it takes is for a close friend to tell me I'm looking awfully tired, or I'm being especially grumpy, and I'm out of here."

Myra's week is typical for our sailors, orchestrating everything at work and home, playing up the contributions of other people while downplaying their own. She works to the point of exhaustion to insure that the job is well done. She reacts strongly when not appreciated for what she has done or when compared unfavorably to others. She takes on so much that a single event at home or at work can upset the equilibrium she values to keep her boat afloat. She is a strong woman, capable of much. But like other sailors, her inclination to overcommit and overdo can interfere with her ability to function well on the job or at home.

Captains in Search of a Crew

Women who are sailors feel confidence in themselves and their abilities. They know their boat, the waters where they sail, and the strengths and weaknesses of their crew. They have the intellect, the vision, and the perseverance to sail alone, but their natural love of people leads them when possible to be part of a team. They seem to choose work settings where they will be responsible not only for their work but also the work of other people. They delight in playing a part in the success of those they teach, mentor, supervise or train. Nothing gives them greater satisfaction than understanding that they have played a significant part in the development or accomplishments of other people. For these reasons they make good administrators capable of getting the work done and fostering good relationships. They make good coaches, able to inspire others to reach higher and dig deeper. They make good counselors and teachers, helping others nurture their strengths and overcome their weaknesses.

It is important that the sailor recruit the right crew to ensure not only a safe smooth sail, but an enjoyable one as well. At times sailors may expect more of one crew member than that person is willing or able to give. In such circumstances, the sailboat captain may blame herself. The problem is her poor leadership or failure to motivate rather than in the individual's shortcomings. Sometimes sailors try too hard to keep a crew member on board when the better decision would be to end the relationship and send the individual on her way. Sailors are slow to admit they can't "save" a crew member from failure. They may allow such a person to delay the progress of the boat.

The crew members may be skilled in sailing or have no experience whatsoever. But the captain, giving detailed, clear directions to each member of the crew, helps each person feel that she has an important part in making things work. At the end of the trip the captain does not claim all the credit. Success is seen as a team effort. But in reality, only one who is knowledgeable and skilled in the ways of the water can be in charge. All members of the crew must respect the leadership of their captain. They must listen closely, obey orders, and pull their weight. At the end of the trip all can feel a sense of accomplishment that the sail was successful.

Don't Make Waves

Sailors in our group are people pleasers. They hesitate to make anyone angry, including those who work for them. They hate confrontation and will work hard to negotiate a smooth ending to conflict. If they sense that the demands of the organization are interfering with the best interest of an individual, they will always protect the person. For example, Trish, a college instructor, offered to limit her own position to ensure a full workload for a junior faculty member whose job was in jeopardy.

Jeanine gave up her successful job at a church because it appeared that conflict over her leadership might cause friction in the congregation. Pleasing others was more important to Jeanine than pleasing herself. Sailors are eager to make everyone feel valued. But, in truth, they also want to have their part in that success acknowledged. They may not seek recognition in their lives, but they are buoyed by the respect and admiration of those they care about.

Susan is an example. She helped her community start an organization for building international friendships. Working with another woman who had previous experience with the organization, she planned their first project. Her cofounder, however, became sick and couldn't continue. Susan picked up the slack and the group arrived safely at its destination, where it was welcomed by the mayor of the community. But as her cofounder went forward to receive the keys to the city, she left Susan behind and said nothing about her part in the planning or success of the trip.

Susan's children were outraged, but Susan chose to

ignore the slight in order to protect the positive atmosphere of the participants. She did, however, warm to the kind words of those who reassured her that they knew who had been responsible for the outcome. The compliments and appreciation of the group and of her children were enough. Susan decided that she had done the right thing, allowing someone to upstage her who obviously needed the recognition more than she did. Like Susan, sailors do not need public recognition, but praise from those important to them is essential. They do want the important people in their lives, whether at work or at home, to be very clear that they can't live without them and that the world would be such a sadder place if they weren't in it!

The sailor's desire to please everyone often leads to overcommitment. Sailors have an exceedingly difficult time saying "no" to anyone. If they have a job where they work closely with people with whom they have significant personal relationships, they will stay in that job if they possibly can, no matter what. Jan, a gifted psychologist, is an example. She was valued as a teacher; respected as a therapist. When her husband's job took him to another city, Jan went with him rather than risk his happiness in his professional life. Jan kept her old job, rather than look for a position close to her new home. During four years she drove thousands of miles, so she wouldn't disappoint those who depended on her work. Only when physical problems made it impossible to continue did she finally quit. Maintaining these friendships and connections seemed worth the inconvenience.

Running on Empty

Sailors will do almost anything for anyone if they feel it serves an important purpose. They take any request seriously as long as it appears to have some meaning attached to it. These women give away their time, their energy, and even their ideas to help a good cause. Whether their generosity may compromise their own chances for success or recognition hardly occurs to them. If they feel that they are helping in the projects they support, they will ignore oversights or slights from coworkers, employers, or their community.

Jackie was an excellent teacher. She designed her courses carefully to meet all the goals of her students. Every minute of class time served a purpose. From years of planning she developed a thick notebook containing outlines for each class, research articles, handouts, transparencies, and resources for teaching. Then one semester she couldn't teach the course. Cheerfully she handed over her notebook to a colleague, so that the quality of the course would not be compromised. Little did she know that soon her colleague would claim ownership not only of the course but also of the notebook's content—all created by Jackie.

The role models that sailors admire are people who also give unselfishly. It may be Mother Teresa or a professor who gave unselfishly so that her female students could reach their potential. In many respects the type of giving that sailors admire is like that of a mother. She is protective, caring, and comforting. She is a nurturer, a motivator, and a confidant. These women brought the best parts of their role as "mother" into the work place as well as the home front.

But there is a down side to this unselfish giving. These women tend to complain of fatigue. In reality, few people know just how much these women do. If you ask them to join in a project, they eagerly come on board with little thought of what personal compromises might have to be made. On the surface they appear to have it all together, but the constant fatigue, the cost of giving so much of themselves both at work and at home, leaves them feeling empty. One such sailor revealed that her ideal vacation would take her completely away from anybody who may want anything from her. These thoughts may be confusing to her family and friends. She dearly loves to be with them, listen to them, party with them, cry with them. Why would she enjoy travel that omitted her friends and family?

Because the exhaustion saps her energy at times, makes her restless and impatient, and sets her up to be irritable with those she loves and cares for.

Sailors who demand too much of themselves may end up feeling defeated in their efforts to do a good job, or be an ideal wife, mother, colleague, boss, sister, or citizen. If a sailor believes it possible to take care of everyone at all times, under any circumstances, and never be tired, upset, angry, or disappointed, her inability to do just that will guarantee unhappiness and fatigue.

Big Crew but only One First Mate

Sailors don't want to be confined in a boat and dependent on others for their safety and security unless they can have crew members they love, like, respect, or admire. So although they are committed with every ounce of their being to those who sail with them, they don't hesitate to point out the ways that their "crew" disappoints them. At home, they have high expectations that their husbands and children will be as loving, ambitious, and committed to their goals as they are. They want men who are strong, ambitious, and intelligent, even superior to them. But they also want to feel that their men can't live without them. They expect their children to work up to their potential, to be loyal, to reflect the family values, and to bring honor to the family in what they do and who they are. Expecting others to work at the same level, to give with the same intensity, can lead to family burnout. If everyone is working too hard, they don't play.

Sailing is a lot of work. It should be taken seriously. But it is also supposed to be a source of relaxation and serenity. Sometimes just allowing the wind to take the boat where it will, enjoying the ride, is enough. One boomer shared the plaintive request of her small daughter who asked her mother if she wouldn't just stop and "sit with me for awhile."

Sometimes You Need a Motor

Sailing conditions can change very quickly, sometimes without warning. The weather may change. Equipment may develop problems. When the wind changes, the crew has to act quickly. Lines must be retied, sails adjusted, direction altered. No one in a position of importance can afford to be slack. In these circumstances changes have to be made quickly and efficiently. To a great degree our sailors set themselves up for this kind of challenge. With so many projects, so many people to please, so many places to perform, difficulties will arise on a fairly consistent basis. The confidence of the captain will help members of the crew remain calm while they make changes. But there are changes and they are constant.

Women who are sailors face multiple demands on their time, at home and in the workplace. If a problem arises, no matter how small, it can be a source of great anxiety for the sailor. Robin had a responsible position as a project director. She was expecting a visit from a regional supervisor that would determine how much money her organization was to receive for her favorite project. She had it all planned. Every piece of information, every person primed for success. Then the telephone rang. Her housekeeper's daughter was in the hospital. Suddenly Robin was in a quandary. She supported her housekeeper's need to be with her own child but she also knew the importance of the job at hand. And Robin was devoted to her own daughter, who was too young to be alone at home without the housekeeper. The situation felt overwhelming to Robin. Fortunately, an older colleague saw her distress and arranged for his wife to go over and care for Robin's daughter until she could get home.

Robin's situation points out the importance of a support system in the lives of the sailors. Just as someone else must be able to take the helm of the boat if the captain becomes disabled, these women need people they can depend on anytime, under any circumstances. Fortunately, these sailors have so often gone beyond the call of duty in helping other people that they have a lot of favors to call in. Many people would help the sailor if she would only ask. When she finally does ask, they are grateful for a chance to feel as important in her life as she is in theirs.

Diversity Makes for an Interesting Crew

Sailing is a sport that appeals to people across the barriers of age, race, profession, and gender. A crew can be composed of many combinations of different people. Their love of sailing and their commitment to performing their role brings them together despite their differences. Likewise, sailors are adaptable and can help other boomer athletes as long as they recognize the purpose or meaning of the task. But this acceptance of a wide range of personalities has its downside. Dealing closely with a variety of people can be draining for sailors. After all, each interaction requires shifting gears. Odds are these acquaintances will take more than they give.

Donna has numerous friends from many of our groups. She finds different kinds of people to be interesting, curious, and fun. But many times the drain on her energy and time leads to frustration and disappointment. Maxine has been a close friend of Donna for many years, or so it seems. Their relationship began when a hurricane disrupted schedules at their office. Maxine was distressed, fearing she could not meet an important deadline with no electricity and support staffers, who were at home struggling to take care of their families. As expected, Donna couldn't resist the need of another. She moved in to rescue Maxine, calming her and offering her the use of portable equipment and her own secretary, who had continued to work. This event set the pattern, with carefully scripted roles ready to be repeated again. Whenever Maxine was overwhelmed, she called upon Donna for encouragement, guidance, and support. Donna was always there. When Maxine needed to make important decisions, she asked Donna for advice. When Maxine felt depressed, Donna cheered her up. Donna became mother superior, father confessor, friend, coach, and confidante, always there for Maxine. But Maxine couldn't do the same for Donna. She had little empathy for what complicated Donna's life. At times she even minimized Donna's importance to her, forgetting appointments or failing to follow through on promises. But Donna couldn't quit. She was needed. Otherwise the winds of torment and suffering might overwhelm Maxine.

Marsha was another of Donna's friends. They shared many of the same professional interests. Marsha gladly talked about work with Donna and readily gave advice, but there was a price. She never allowed Donna to own her own professional triumphs. Instead, she slipped into her compliments the suggestion that Donna couldn't have succeeded without Marsha's help. There were even times when Marsha insulted Donna. But Donna endured slights because the friendship was longstanding. She saw Marsha's shortcomings as humorous. But Donna paid a price. It wore on her to maintain a relationship in which she had to be guarded, in which she gave more than she got.

Don't Give Up the Ship

Loyalty is a cardinal virtue to sailors. Abandoning the ship is unthinkable. They may stay even when it's sinking. Sailors tend to have long-term relationships and forgive old friends. They try to mend broken relationships, assuming responsibility—even when there is none—for causing the problems. They can hate the trouble, and love the troublemaker. When relationships go sour, they are deeply hurt and obsess about what happened and why, alternating between anger and feelings of rejection. They will go to any lengths to try to heal wounds with a colleague, friend, or spouse, even when it is beyond repair.

Dawn was married to a man she found enchanting. She had dated many men and had received more than a few proposals. But he was intriguing, different from anyone she had ever known. She was in love. Determined to live her life with him, she set a course to win his heart. They married, and she gave the marriage her all. She forsook her friends, jeopardized her health, compromised her values, and still was betrayed in the end. She wanted to be married so badly, she loved him so completely, that she sacrificed everything for him. Unfortunately, he didn't deserve her love, didn't appreciate her loyalty, and didn't regret being a jerk. The relationship ran aground. Even Dawn, so skilled at sailing, couldn't get it unstuck. Typical of a sailor, she quit only when it was hopeless.

Sailors will appear to lack good judgment at times because they are willing to get involved with people and situations that can be destructive. Resiliency allows them to try again, whether in the same relationship or another. They trust that things will turn out to their advantage, if they just keep working long enough. They have long-term relationships of all types. Only one of our sailors had divorced; most had been married for over twenty years. Sailors describe friends that they have had since childhood or college. Even though they don't see them often, they nurture the relationships through telephone calls, visits, and the celebration of important events.

Sailing is a Lifelong Sport

Our sailors are ambivalent about retirement. As long as they see a way to be involved with meaningful projects and with people they enjoy, they want to continue to make a contribution—whether they are paid for it or not. The success they have had at home and at work gives them confidence that they will find their niche in the community. Just as real sailors enjoy sailing until their health prohibits it, our boomer sailors relish being part of life's mainstream as long as they have the desire. But if their children or grandchildren need them, they are likely to find ways to compromise their work life to help them accomplish their goals.

Their lives have strong patterns: finding joy in working with others toward shared goals; putting aside their own needs to serve others; caring little for outside praise but savoring the love and admiration of those they love and protect. These women are highly satisfied with their lives. Perhaps the key has been their ability to have it all at work and at home, to be successful in both arenas, loving the relationships as well as the work. These women have adapted the roles of mother and wife for their career paths. In both places, they have found ways to use their feminine traits of connectedness and devotion to relationships. Sailing. It's not an easy sport, but a highly pleasurable one.

Chapter 8

THE MARTIAL ARTIST

"Peaceful Warriors"

Rachel moves back from the microphone, allowing Sally to make the final remarks. She has great respect and admiration for her colleague who has spent so much of her time and talent supporting causes Rachel holds dear. She feels gratified by the energy and enthusiasm of the crowd and prays it will translate into action leading to change. She loves these women who have joined together in a cause. The possibilities seem endless. Her face radiates happiness and fulfillment.

Sally concludes her remarks with a brilliant recap of the conference agenda. She is relieved that it is finally coming to a close and she can escape the crowd. Her body is taut, her face strained. One more minute of this and she might explode. As the applause dies down, she searches for a chance to escape.

"How about dinner?" she hears Rachel ask.

"Thanks, but I've still got work to do," Sally quickly replies.

"Oh, okay. Well, take care of yourself."

"I know what that means," Sally thinks. "You look terrible. You're too thin. You need to get more rest. The truth is that if Rachel were half as committed as I am, she might lose weight, feel tired more often, and even give up those little dinners with friends."

But Sally doesn't betray her thoughts. She smiles warmly at Rachel, clasping her hand before she turns to leave. Sally finds Rachel tiresome. Her everlasting optimism and good humor irritate her. They may be on the same team, but only in cause and conscience, not in heart and soul. Sally doesn't like Rachel. In fact, she really doesn't like many people at all. She keeps most of those around her at arms length, glad for the fact that her intensity intimidates them.

Sally and Rachel are both activists. They spend their professional lives and much of their personal energy promoting causes they think are important. These causes may be for those less fortunate, children, other women, or for the protection of the things they value such as the environment or political rights. Whatever the cause, they are devoted disciples to their mission. They are much like disciples of the martial arts. They train for the contest, disciplining themselves to achieve their goals. They are single-minded as they focus on the target, not concerning themselves with anything but the opponent. Often they sacrifice personal time with family and friends who, recognizing the value of their work, don't complain. They are willing to go alone, if necessary, to confront the opponent, or they can work as part of a team with each score adding to the overall chances of success.

Advocate or Warrior

Martial arts require training, discipline, and patience. Students must use their cunning, intellect, and fast reflexes to beat their opponents. This is also true for the women we interviewed who champion a cause. At one extreme, they may be "advocates" with a missionary zeal to lift up the underdog, driven by a spiritual vision or experience. At the other extreme, activists can be "warriors,'" motivated by their own pain, aiming to score a victory in the war with oppressors of the underdog. Most activists are somewhere in between the two poles.

Sally and Rachel represent the two extremes. Underneath the elaborately scripted rituals of their day-to-day work, they differ in intent and emotion. Rachel is the advocate and feels her work is a mission. She is motivated by humanitarian values that make her efforts meaningful. She does not seek material gain as much as the personal satisfaction of giving her time and talents for something significant.

Sally is the warrior. She is driven by the need to prove she has the power to make things happen. She does what she does not so much because it is a "good" thing to do, but because it is the "right" thing to do. Forces that have hardened her to the world have shaped her attitude. If she has power, which may also mean money, then she is happy. Power, status and money do not disappoint her as much as people might. In her mind, no one can take these away. People come and go. Power endures. Seeing her name on a CEO nameplate, on a book, on a program, in a newspaper article make her feel like a success. Fortunately for those she chooses to champion, she is very good at what she does. Unfortunately for her, she does not get the kind of personal rewards that could, in fact, alleviate the underlying disappointment she feels from her life.

Consider the movie, "The Karate Kid." Mr. Miago is a karate master and a decorated soldier. He agrees to train Daniel, not for revenge against the bullies who have made Daniel's life miserable, but so that he might gain respect for himself by withstanding their blows. In the process, he teaches Daniel about life as well as karate. Be patient. Things are not always as they seem. Use karate only for defense and when it is the last option. Always look your opponent in the eye. Discipline yourself. Learn the basics. Mr. Miago trains Daniel for the tournament in which he will have the opportunity to defend himself. As he does, he helps Daniel see himself differently, as a winner, not a loser, and as someone who can face a problem and not feel compelled to hide. During the competition, Daniel's opponents cheat, injuring him in ways that would make it impossible in most cases to continue. Mr. Miago, an advocate, encourages Daniel, watching him as he draws upon his lessons and makes the decision not to back down. He finds a legal way to beat his enemy with grace and style, not with anger and revenge. The final scene shows the bully handing Daniel the trophy, joining in the cheers for the new champion.

Another sensei master at the local karate school, a warrior, is a contrast to Mr. Miago. This instructor alternates between humiliating his students and teaching them to "have no mercy" toward each other. His face is marked with anger and hostility. Every threat to his role or his goals is met with sarcasm. He appears driven by a need not just to defeat, but to break the spirit of his opponent. During the tournament, he demands that they cheat in order to win. Even then, when winning is not assured, he instructs his student to injure Daniel rather than take any chance that he might not win. His lessons are to be victorious at all costs, never to let your opponent get the upper hand, to destroy those who oppose you, and to be loyal to him, not the rules of the game. In the end, his student deserts him, choosing no longer to be a pawn in his master's selfish desire for dominance.

Both of these men are karate masters but they represent two vastly different approaches in terms of who they are and how they teach. Mr. Miago learned karate from his father who taught him patience, generosity of spirit, empathy, and a love of nature. The other sensei master probably had a very different upbringing from Mr. Miago. The karate that both men practice is an expression of who they are. Martial artists and boomer women who share similar approaches reflect these predispositions in their lives as they work for causes.

Janice is an advocate who is a talented writer and performer. Her teachers and parents strongly encouraged her to pursue a career on stage, but her devotion to her family and her faith led her in a different direction. Instead of seeking fame for herself, she saw a larger need in the young people of her church who needed a firm spiritual foundation. She felt strongly that more grounding would be essential for them to become healthy, well-adjusted adults. She decided to focus her energies to help them in this way by becoming a published author and consultant for churches. She wonders at times what her life would have been like had she made different decisions. But she says, "The progress I have seen in church programming and the positive changes in the youth I work with remind me constantly of the 'greater good' to which I am committed."

Marta, on the other hand, is a warrior. She is driven by the need to protect those who might fall victim to the same abuse that she suffered as a child. Her mother had so little trust in her that she took her for an abortion when she wasn't even pregnant. Her father was mostly absent and when he was home verbally abused and terrorized his family. Marta is angry about what she has endured. She has channeled this anger into protecting children from suffering the same experiences she has had. Identifying closely with the plight of the abused and neglected child, she is a soldier in a war against a society or any family that allows children to be hurt. But Marta suffers. She cannot overcome the pain of self-doubt and low self-esteem her childhood inflicted on her. No matter how many children she protects and saves, she carries the daily burden of her own wounds.

Whether warrior or advocate, all activists want a better world. They mean well, whether their style suggests desires to subdue oppressors or to empower others to defend themselves. In her book, *The Intuitive Body*, Wendy Palmer describes aikido as "a unique martial art which holds as its ideal the intent to love and protect all beings, even those who attack with intent to harm." This is also true for boomer martial artists. Professionally, they choose fields such as the ministry, medicine, politics, and counseling. They lend themselves to being able to focus on defending the vulnerable and defenseless. One of our boomer women who was a physician said, "I love to work with policy related to healthcare because I can impact more people that way. I can do more in writing one large grant than I can working with one patient at a time in the clinic. My goal is to make big changes as fast as possible for as many as possible."

IQ or EQ

Clearly, you have to be smart to make the many changes most activists seek. But activists often need people skills and emotional maturity as well. To influence key people they have to blend these two factors to have as much impact as they want. Advocates tend to have this blend; often warriors don't.

Warriors rely on speed, cunning, and strategy to win. They have no time for sentimentality. Empathy is unnecessary and counterproductive. To concern herself about how the opponent might feel or how a blow might hurt would cause this fighter to lose ground, literally, and allow her adversary to gain the advantage.

Darlene was a lobbyist for children's rights. To gain support for her work, she often spoke to civic groups, church gatherings, or town meetings. In these forums, she often found herself becoming more and more emotional over the children she cared for so much. During one session, she alienated a potential ally by protesting that "Americans don't really care about kids. If they did, there would never again be a child who suffered harassment in his or her own school. Surely a country that can put a man on the moon can protect its children!" An attorney who happened to be on the school board was in the audience. He had recently been criticized for his soft stand on welfare issues. Immediately after Darlene made her pronouncement, she read the awkward reaction of the audience and remembered the attorney was present. She quickly added a disclaimer that it was not always easy to be sure a situation was truly one of harassment, but the damage was done. The embarrassed attorney shunned her. The effectiveness of Darlene's convincing speech was compromised by being oblivious to who was in the audience.

Advocates are more likely to consider the feelings and concerns of their opponents and tend to see those who differ from themselves as needy, not nasty. They need information. They need to be made aware of the errors in their thinking and it is the advocates' job to provide these things. They work hard to win over the opposition and reap some of the peace and tranquility through the process that the advocates treasure. They understand that aggression stems from fear. They know that it is better to embrace the enemy, admit to your own and the opponents' darker side, and seek enlightenment for all.

Martyr or Mask

Jan hurried off the stage. It had been a grueling 14-hour day that included a speech to 1400 people, meeting with legislative bodies, responding to questions from the media, and preparing for the next day's conference events. The very next day, she would be receiving an honorary doctorate at one of the most prestigious universities in the nation. It should have been a great time for her, but all she felt was tired. She turned down an invitation with the conference organizers sure that more hours of socializing would be tedious. "They will have a million questions about my work and how things stand and it will feel more like an interview than fun to me," she said. "These kinds of dinners always leave me feeling drained of my intellect, energy, and creativity, anyway. Those people seem to always take, never give." Exhausted, she ordered from room service and fell asleep before she finished her meal. The next morning, she appeared on time, prepared, astute and with a ready handshake for everyone she encountered. To those she met and the many in the audience, she appeared the consummate professional, renowned, revered and respected.

A warrior protects herself, keeping her emotions hidden. On the surface, she seems independent, secure, and savvy. But underneath she's often a lonely, discontent, and dissatisfied woman. She interacts with many people, but is close to few or none. The need to protect herself prevents anyone from really knowing her. The time and energy it would take to combat her paranoia and fears of intimacy would distract from her work. And work, after all, is the real source of a warrior's feelings of strength and worth.

The women interviewed who fell into this group described childhoods where love was conditional. When young and vulnerable, they did not feel understood or consistently nurtured. In some cases, it was a parent who was unable or unwilling to meet the child's needs. Eleanor describes the pain of enduring the "silent treatment" from her father. If she did not do exactly as he wished, he punished her by acting as if she did not exist. In other cases, the child may have been so different from the parent that the natural loving instincts of the parents were stifled. Frances parents' were uneducated, simple people. Their daughter, a gifted, intense prodigy, seemed so mature that they treated her like an adult rather than the child that she was. Sadly she suffered the loss of her childhood.

Advocates do not use the same strategies as warriors. They actually embrace their opponents as they embrace their causes, hoping to bring balance to the situation and if not, to learn something from their failures. They are not afraid to lose. They possess what the author Wendy Palmer refers to as the "tentra," the part of the self that knows real satisfaction from entering the energetic middle of life rather than standing back and observing. This guides the martial artist to engage rather than to defend or attack. The boomer advocates we interviewed are not afraid to show their emotions. They do not fear that they will be hurt as they pursue their agendas. The importance of their mission is so great they feel satisfaction that, at least, they are suffering for a good cause. They stay open to the many possibilities that the combination of work and change can create and they have nothing to hide.

Imperfect Perfectionism

As forgiving as they are of those they try to help, activists, especially warriors, have a low tolerance for personal mistakes.

Warriors are perfectionists and demand perfection in those around them. They have little or no patience for an administrative staff that is less intelligent, less perceptive, or less intense than they are.

JoAnne is a nationally known spokesperson for environmental clean-up. She's in demand for her writing, lecturing, teaching, and consulting. Anyone familiar with her field knows her and her prolific work. Major universities jockey for the right to "own" her as part of their faculty. Once she becomes an esteemed member of their faculty, they find that she is not the easiest person to satisfy. She requires extensive secretarial support, demands time away from class to give lectures and to consult, and resents being asked to participate on committees. Fiercely guarding her time, she spares little for the university "family" that feels so fortunate to have her. JoAnne consistently requires that others around her remain flexible in the face of her inflexibility. She wants all of the control but complains that she has none. She feels that her many contributions to the institution should result in special treatment. She constantly pushes the limit on what others are able to provide. More often than not, all of her demands are not only met but exceeded, since the recognition she brings to the university is usually worth what it pays to keep her.

A pattern always develops. If it seems to her that the demands being placed on her are excessive, she becomes resentful, angry and restless. "I'm no happier at this university than I was at the other one," JoAnne complains. She equates unmet demands with a lack of respect, which affects her self-esteem. Ultimately, she goes too far and asks for too much. Rejection signals that it is time to search elsewhere for the elusive setting that would bring her peace. It seems that no setting can meet her needs and she has moved to several universities over time. She doesn't realize she fights for the protection of some while easily assaulting the people around her trying to do the same good work. She's become a "prima donna" even though she presses for better treatment for all. Sadly, JoAnne can't see the contradictions in her own behavior.

The advocates we interviewed are the opposite. They are very democratic, perhaps even self-effacing. They ask little for themselves. Of course, they can go too far. They may deplete their energies by taking on many of the mundane tasks in their work in addition to the responsibilities for the larger picture. They don't want to "bother" the others around them. In some cases, they may even lose some of their power by refusing to take credit for the work that they do. Karen was always uncomfortable asking her secretary to prepare materials she needed for meetings. "It's better for me to do it and make sure that it gets done right," she rationalizes. "Besides I can do it faster and better."

If you aren't with me, you're against me."

Kathy was a tireless fighter for children's rights. She was complimented when her supervisor asked her to follow him to another job so he might benefit from her work. She was successful in working with children and in creating change in the systems that served them. During a particularly stressful time in her personal life, she became sarcastic and demeaning to a group of school personnel. They became frustrated and complained to her supervisor, who criticized her for her behavior and told her to go back and mend fences with the school people. She refused, forcing him to use an outside consultant to cool tensions between the school and his program. Kathy became confused, resentful and lost face with the school and faith in her supervisor. "I was right," she insisted. "How could he let them attack me?" Ultimately, she quit her job, maintaining she could not forgive the betrayal she experienced by her supervisor.

Because warriors have tunnel vision over their mission, they tend to see things through their own set of expectations and can't see the perspectives of others. If disagreements arise with co-workers, they hold a grudge, even to the point of quitting. People they work with may feel personally attacked. The warrior is so aggressive that co-workers may feel a need to retaliate or defend themselves. This reaction usually confuses the fighter who does not realize that she comes across this way. "Why, when I work so hard, would anyone be so mean to me?" one pleaded to us.

It is no accident that warriors do not have role models. No one could live up the idealized version of the person they can admire. They sabotage relationships by pushing harder and harder to test their loyalty. Because even their admiring friends or co-workers are human, they will inevitably disappoint them and they end up alone—again. Cross a warrior and you are relegated to the ranks of the discarded. They want so much for someone to love them, entertain them, relieve them of some of the burden of responsibility, but their own intensity and uncompromising nature make them high maintenance friends and co-workers.

Winners at work; Losers at home

These women are amazing in terms of the incredible feats they accomplish with their causes. They are professionally successful by almost anyone's definition. But no matter how miraculous these feats, they are never enough to overcome their loneliness and isolation or the warrior's lack of self-esteem. They want to be cherished and prized. Interestingly, they often are drawn to the very relationships that cannot, for one reason or another, provide this for them. Instead of finding people, particularly men, who will value and support them, they seek out those who need protecting, championing, and nurturing. Such men may appear to be proponents of their causes, but over time, prove to lack the courage, skill or the insight of the activist. Consider Hillary Clinton who has worked hard to promote many focused causes. One of the things that most attracted her to her husband was how they both wanted to take on the world and make it better. Unfortunately, her husband's philandering tripped her up. Still she stands by her man and does everything to make him a success. But her battle, just like that of activists like her, is as real at home as it is on the streets, or in war-torn countries, or where families are suffering. To do what she wanted to do, she had to continue to support him, putting her own priorities aside.

Children can also cause stress and disappointment. One activist admitted that her son gave her fits, getting into trouble. She worried that her being gone so much, trying to help others had contributed to the problem. "I just didn't have anything left when I got home," she recalls. "Fighting other people's battles all day, I had no energy for any at home." In some cases, this guilt can make disciplining children difficult. Monitoring their behavior and punishing kids is just too emotionally taxing. Jenine shakes her head as she confesses, "Sure, I overlooked some of his antics. I didn't want all of our time together to be unpleasant."

One advocate said with a certain degree of pride that she had spent much time talking to her children about the work she was doing. When possible, she also tried to involve them in projects. For example, Jackie often took her three children with her when she went to the homeless shelter—especially when she had tasks that involved homeless children. "It's important for them to learn first-hand how hard life can be for those less fortunate." In this case, her children saw her work as part of something bigger than themselves, a mission of making the world a better place. Rather than feeling excluded, they had a sense of ownership. These children follow their mother's footsteps and have become part of advocacy groups on their own. They feel pride in her accomplishments and have learned valuable lessons about unselfishness, commitment and devotion to duty from her model.

Off-center

Martial artists rely on no one but themselves. They are individualists who do not trust institutions that are made up of human beings to meet their needs. Warriors, in particular, expect people to make mistakes, to fail to follow through on assignments, to fail to support them, and ultimately to interfere with the success of their programs.

Lori was a committed professional, whose expertise was the emotionally handicapped preschooler. When her church called upon her to help strengthen the early childhood components of its program, she quickly agreed to build a preschool. Her job as Director of a day treatment program for emotionally disturbed young people motivated her to start an early intervention center for high risk children. The church's commitment to the program led her to believe that this was not only a project that needed doing but that this was a church she would be comfortable joining. The program flourished and the church felt like home. But it wasn't to last.

The leadership of the church changed and support for the project diminished. Some church members even began to question Lori's leadership. They decided to set up a board to govern the program, allowing her to attend but not to have a vote. She began to feel uncomfortable with the anger she felt toward the church for not recognizing the crucial part she had played in the success of the center. The last straw came when she recommended a friend for a key position and the board rejected her because she was African-American. This sealed Lori's decision to leave not only the center, but the church as well. She gave up her church family, feeling justifiably self-righteous in her decision. True, she could have challenged the church about its discomfort with diversity. Perhaps she, as well as the church, might have grown from the process. But like many activists, Lori did not trust the system to change.

Activists we interviewed generally describe themselves as spiritual, but not religious. They value moral principles and seek out spiritual sources of inspiration, but they are unlikely to join a church. These institutions are far too flawed for their tastes. They prefer the safety of spiritual inspiration and nourishment through reading, retreats, and meditation.

Illustrating a true kinship to the principles of martial arts, several said that the philosophy of Zen holds great appeal. This philosophy teaches that life is not a series of goals to be achieved but a path to be walked for its own sake. Said one woman: "This is a lifestyle for me. I'm just trying to be a 'good' person and fix things that are broken. I try to be more forgiving of the systems that are in place, accepting that they are not perfect. But to me the best way to be 'good' is to be true to myself and work with the issues that I think need the most attention. I live with this in mind every day."

Retirement or Retreat

Activists don't consider retirement. They value their work much more than their personal lives and see the two as wrapped up together. Most have no concrete plans to retire and certainly would not consider it without the financial means to be independent. Used to staying on the go, they do fear that once they scale back, they might not have enough to do. Their value and worth as human beings are based on their ability to win one more war for someone. Their "being" is in their "doing." In the Karate Kid, Mr. Miago experienced new life in his relationship as a mentor to Daniel. In the same way, activists are considering redefining their playing fields, finding missions that can be part of their lives. One, a university professor said, "I recognize that I just don't have the same energy to do it all anymore. Doing the fieldwork and trying to get volunteers to follow-up plus teaching the courses is overkill. Perhaps I can plant a seed in my students and they will take up the cause." Regardless of how and where they decide to do it, these women express the clear intention to look for ways to feel the same exhilaration they experience when they are part of making the world a better place.

Chapter 9

THE MOUNTAIN CLIMBER

"Reaching the Summit"

TAKING a rare day off from her position as dean of a graduate business school, Marie stood at the foot of Mount Rainier with her two nieces. She was excited, glad that she had turned down a lucrative consulting opportunity for today's hike. She loved climbing mountains, especially ones so high that on cloudy days she couldn't even see the top. Today her destination would be only a short distance up an easy trail. But she always daydreamed about going all the way up, knowing the summit was there just waiting for her arrival. While it might seem like an unrealistic goal for someone who was not an accomplished mountaineer, she knew that it was just a matter of time before she would gaze down upon the Seattle area from the clouds.

Going beyond people's expectations was nothing new for Marie. She was a determined and driven person even as a young girl—a classic perfectionist. Aiming for straight A's on her report card, she would stay up hours past her bedtime doing and re-doing each assignment until it was flawless. She learned early to set specific and very high goals for herself—even if some seemed out of reach for her capabilities—and simply make them happen. As a young professional, when asked if she was Miss or Mrs., she would say "Dr." and smile. Though she was years from becoming one, she knew that was who she wanted to be someday.

Marie came from a family of public school professionals and everyone assumed that she would become a teacher. She chose, however, the field of business, which was a much riskier decision in her parents' view. She began as a sales representative for a large corporation, traveling constantly, routinely working 70-80 hours a week, and sacrificing vacations to stay ahead of her workload. It was a stressful life, but she was relentless in her pursuit to be the best. She knew she wanted to be on top, but at this point she wasn't sure what "on top" meant. She did know that the road ahead was going to be long and hard. Her daily emotions vacillated between unbridled hope that it would all be worth it and a sense of dread for what it would cost her to make the climb. Reassurance came when early efforts resulted in her being the first woman in her company awarded "Rookie of the Year."

Her accomplishments were noticed, although not always appreciated, by some of her highly competitive male peers who resented being bested by a woman. But no one could deny the amount and quality of her work. As the only female, she often felt totally alone and wondered if there was a better, less painful, way of going about all of this. She longed for a female role model or at least one female co-worker with whom she could commiserate and who might offer support. Instead, she discovered that this would be the first of many situations during the next three decades where SHE would be a "trailblazer" for many women who were entering a male-dominated field. Fate had assigned her the task of guiding hundreds of female climbers up the mountain. In effect, she would spend her entire career becoming the role model for others that she had so wanted and needed herself.

*　　*　　*

Marie is our mountain climber. Those who participate in this dangerous sport are known for their legendary strength and drive. According to Jon Krakauer, the author of **Into Thin Air**, who recounted a Mount Everest disaster in 1996, mountain climbers have to throw caution to the winds. They must ignore the fears of those they love and willingly subject themselves to danger. They live for the "high" they will experience when they arrive at the peak. Women in this group understand this and they set extremely high goals and remain relentless in their pursuit of them. Likewise, they energetically tackle the many smaller "peaks" that they encounter along the way—each one representing an intermediate feat in its own right. They demonstrate an uncompromising commitment to a goal. Why would anyone choose such a hard road and scale a mountain? "Because it is there," according to T.K. Mallory, the famous climber of Mount Everest in the 1920's. These women give the same answer.

Many baby boom women in the late 60's selected a profession that was somewhat traditional, usually a choice that would not interfere too much with their ability also to be good wives and mothers. In contrast, mountain climbers deliberately sought more unconventional career challenges. Most of the women we interviewed in this group said that the first priority in their twenties and thirties was to focus on a career, although they admitted that periodically relationships and children shared center stage as well. If they did choose traditional careers, they rarely followed the crowd. They "marched to the beat of their own drummers" and carved out new approaches to doing them.

In the extreme, baby boom mountain climbers are either workaholics or entrepreneurs. The task-oriented workaholics among them are driven by the all-consuming desire to reach the top at all costs. Their days are packed with back-to-back activities and meetings, as well as travel in many cases. They rise early, work late, often eat lunch at their desks (unless they have a lunch meeting), and spend countless hours at the computer or on the phone. Family, and even guests in their homes, must be prepared to spend "quality time" with them during rare pockets of time that these mountain climbers assign for "relaxation." Even then, it is not unusual for plans to be altered because "something came up at work."

On the other hand, our entrepreneurs don't have the same game plan. Just as focused and determined to make their mark as the workaholics, they have a different style of tackling the mission. They try to make situations work to their advantage, using incredible people skills to capitalize on the gifts and contributions of others. They cannot only "work a crowd," they find genuine pleasure in doing so. They are affable and popular and will more often than not try to mix business with pleasure. Through imaginative gatherings, these friendly movers and shakers know how to schmooze. Most mountain climbers we interviewed are somewhere in between the workaholics and the entrepreneurs. They construct their own combination of these two extremes to create something that works for them. Regardless, it is safe to say that all mountain climbers are ambitious perfectionists who are multi-talented risk-takers. Marie (the workaholic) and Toby (an entrepreneur) best represent the extremes.

Visible but Invisible

Toby is a classic example of an entrepreneur who has cleverly mastered the complex nature of corporate America, reaching the top of the ladder of a major manufacturing company. She defied many odds and endured countless difficulties as she bumped into the glass ceiling repeatedly during her thirty years in business. She is now a senior vice-president and supervises many groups and individuals, mostly men, who actually have more paper credentials than she. This is no small feat for an African-American woman in the South who started with this company at the bottom of the ladder just out of college. But she saw exciting potential for breaking new ground there. Armed with a clear vision of where she was going and a relentless determination not to be deterred, she achieved her dream.

Toby knew as a college student in the sixties that she wanted a life different from that of her friends. She came from an unusual family for the time; she was the fourth generation to attend college. Her parents instilled in her ambition, confidence and self-reliance and provided her with constant love and support along the way. Predictably, she graduated at the top of her class in high school. As a freshman at her parents'and grandparents' alma mater, she crafted a deliberate plan for her future—she was going to make a difference in this world. The first step to accomplish this would be to prepare for and land an important job doing something she enjoyed and thought was important. She correctly reasoned that she would be able to write her own ticket if she majored in one of the sciences. She liked chemistry, although it was not even her best subject and, upon graduation, she accepted one of the seven positions she was offered as junior research chemist with a large company.

As an African-American woman in a white, "good ole boy" environment, Toby found that she was visible, yet invisible. She was treated politely for the most part, and she was definitely noticed, but for years, she carried little influence. She suffered a variety of disappointments along the way—some bigger than others. But each one seemed to strengthen her resolve to rise to the top, no matter how hard or uncomfortable it was.

Her incredible willpower was evident in an episode that occurred in the early 1980's. She and other representatives from her company were meeting with another company to firm up the particulars of a major collaboration. She was the only woman, as well as the only African-American, in a group of 100 white men used to opening the meetings with some sort of joke. The head of the other company did not notice her and proceeded to tell a story about "the little colored girl." Everyone froze, casting awkward glances her way. She and everyone else knew that this uncomfortable exchange could potentially be a deal breaker. To put everyone at ease, she got up and walked over to him, saying, "Here I is!" She then laughed and everyone else joined in. Everyone was grateful to her for saving the day, but she admitted that she went home afterwards and cried for two days. Yet she did what she felt she had to do—go along to get along. She knew she would win in the end and she vowed not let these men keep her from obtaining what she wanted—respect and recognition for what she could contribute. Toby's pleasant and warm personality has been her most effective tool which has enabled her consistently to stay on good terms with people at all levels in the company for more than three decades.

One Focus/Many Foci

Toby and Marie have always been focused. In many ways, mountain climbers, especially ones like Marie, are solitary personalities whose goal provides meaning and purpose in life. Their primary goal is always one that they have identified or designed for themselves and, more than likely, one that has not been attempted by any or many before them. Whether it is to reach the top of Mount Everest or to become the presidents of their own companies, these climbers never lose sight of the goal. The mission becomes all consuming and other aspects of their lives are second. Although they often find themselves in unfamiliar territory, they know what is possible and they won't be deterred. An Everest climber once said, "I'd failed to appreciate the grip climbing had on my soul or the purpose it lent to my otherwise rudderless life." So too with these women.

This obsession with reaching the top is, of course, the primary appeal of the sport and the ambitions of climbers are so strong that they brush aside any doubts about success. They possess great faith in their abilities, uncommon drive, and remarkable endurance. They are invigorated by the process of stretching themselves in every way, defying the odds of success.

Marie told us she "always feels the need to test myself in everything I do—to push the limit. That's when I feel the most alive."

Like their mountain climbing sisters, Marie is the consummate visionary who is motivated by unique projects that reflect quality and attention to detail. She also does not hesitate to reject the limitations of accepted practice in any form if it threatens to hold her back. Regardless of how uncomfortable, stressful or difficult any obstacles are, mountain climbers will overcome them. They must stay in excellent shape for the ordeal and invest in the right equipment. Likewise, if a higher degree is needed to move to the next level in their career, women in this group get it, whether or not they actually enjoy being in school. If moving to a different city to take a position on the way to the top is required, they go. If taking on extra responsibilities in one work situation will help them get a better job, they take them on. These decisions are essential "equipment" needed for the climb.

Marie realized in her late thirties that she would need a doctorate if she was to move from the work of business to the teaching of business in a college setting—her lifelong dream. She knew it would take leaving a lucrative job and moving half way across the country to enroll into the best program possible. It would also mean convincing her husband of this plan and asking for his support. She was determined to complete the grueling program in less than three years in order to stay on the schedule she had set for herself. The ordeal put tremendous strain on her health and her marriage. But it was a necessary sacrifice she was willing to make that would move her closer to the next "peak" on the trek up her mountain.

As if conquering a mountain isn't demanding enough, these women are simultaneously involved in numerous hobbies and interests that are unrelated to the overall goal. They simply can't sit still for long. Marie is an accomplished seamstress, excellent cook and does her own gardening and yard work, which is substantial. She makes her own yogurt as well as the drapes and decorations for all of the homes she and her husband have built and designed themselves over the years. She is an avid sailor, works out daily, and loves to volunteer time with young people. She spent many years as a Girl Scout leader, adding a weekly meeting plus many camping trips to her already packed schedule. One friend, only half-jokingly, asked her if she suffered from Attention Deficit Disorder. These women work hard, plunging into each project the same intensity and attention to detail they give to everything. Nothing is too much for them.

Relationships are Important—As Long As They Don't Get in the Way

When asked about career versus relationships, the women who fell most clearly into the workaholic category claimed that both were extremely important. They admitted, however, that their life and career decisions reflected a pattern of putting the "mission" first most of the time and fitting people around it. But, they didn't always start out that way. In their early twenties, many of these women described themselves as relationship-oriented, even "pleasers" who actually tried too hard to make others happy. Ultimately, they experienced gradual shifts in their priorities as the result of disappointments in relationships and impatience due to waiting for gratification that never seemed to come.

Marie married Randy, her high school sweetheart, when they graduated from college. Although she had plans to begin her own career, he was a pilot in the military. So she put her own dreams on hold and went with him to live in Korea for several years. He was gone constantly and withdrawn and uncommunicative when he was home with her. Lonely and isolated, she poured her energy into their home. With her usual perfectionism, she agonized over every detail of each project for the house. She planned interesting dinners, trips and social occasions for both of them to enjoy each time he returned from an assignment. Unfortunately, he was a self-centered man with little appreciation for her or her efforts. Once, while he was away for two weeks, she worked night and day to surprise him for his birthday with a completely re-decorated den of his own filled with his favorite things. When he arrived home, he brushed past the big bow on the door, put his things down and said nothing. Marie knew in her heart that she could take no more. It hurt too much to stay in this marriage any longer.

Marie was learning the mountain climber's need to shed unnecessary baggage in order to reach the top. The venture alone is hard enough and the obstacles are already almost impossible to overcome without extra baggage. These women can't allow themselves to be slowed down. So they often give relationships (husbands, friends) less importance if they interfere with their mission. It is not unusual to hear them say of an estranged husband "I outgrew him" or, more charitably, "We grew apart."

Toby, on the other hand, considers her relationship with her family, especially her husband, as the most important thing in her life. They met soon after college and formed a strong, trusting bond that has endured through the years. The two of them are together constantly and she routinely includes him in almost everything she does socially, describing him as her best friend. She feels that balance is the ultimate purpose in her life and that achieving great things at work and on the home front are dual objectives. She has also always been extremely close to her parents who referred to her as "their golden child." She stopped at nothing to make their last days the best possible. While juggling the demanding workload with the company, she threw a "party" for her father every day when he was in the hospital before he died, calling friends and asking them to send him cards to cheer him up. Some days he received up to 40 cards, each one bringing a smile. Being the mountain climber that she is, she knows that she must shed baggage to reach the top. But to her, people in her life are rarely the baggage.

To some, workaholic mountain climbers can appear cold or distant at times, much more task-oriented than people-oriented. However, they don't see themselves that way at all. They are always attentive to co-workers and friends, remembering birthdays and reciprocating when they receive kindnesses. They intend to be warm. As in everything they do, they want to do things right and thus sometimes appear methodically to "check off the boxes" in terms of dealing with others. In truth, they often would prefer to spend most of their time working alone on some new exciting enterprise, but they also want to be perceived as "people persons." Like everyone, they want to be liked. But they clearly feel the strongest connections with others who are also mountain climbers and understand the thrill of reaching a peak where they can soar with eagles. While they may enjoy those who don't share this dream, it is harder for them to respect people who aren't motivated in the same way.

The issue of trust is critical in how these women form relationships. Mountain climbers trying to reach the top of the highest mountains must be very selective in terms of whom they trust. They literally are putting their lives in the hands of the other climbers. One misstep can result in death. This is also true for the women in this group who are consistently focused and serious about their plans and the means they have developed to get where they want to be. The stakes are high in terms of making decisions about whom to trust and they constantly feel that a mistake in this regard can result in significant damage, whether professional or emotional.

Entrepreneurs are more laid back where their personal relationships are concerned. They thrive on the stimulation of mixing with friends. They find that time with friends is not only a pleasant diversion from their busy work schedule but also a source of ideas and innovations they may incorporate into a new venture. They are outgoing and trust their instincts in terms of choosing friends who will help them and provide comfort if things go wrong. They know how to be good friends to others and are appreciated by them. They also are not nearly as devastated as workaholics when relationships turn sour. Toby wears with pride a beautiful bracelet her friends gave her as a "thank you" for all she does for them. Yes, people are a risk but she knows that without them, getting what she wants out of life will be much harder.

Everyone's Entitled to My Own Opinion

Mountain climbers cannot afford the luxury of second-guessing their deliberate and carefully constructed strategy. Tentativeness can be costly and they must keep moving forward. When they have finally defined the approach they need to take, there is little or no room for changing or modifying their plans unless they can be convinced that it is absolutely necessary. They don't *think* they are right about how to do it—they *know* they are. Therefore, some don't respond well to criticism and they resist compromise. They are the epitome of self-reliance and confidence.

Several women in the workaholic category indicated that they didn't see themselves as having much of a sense of humor. That's not to say they don't laugh or aren't amused by situations, but "being silly" does not come naturally to them in most circumstances. This is consistent with a sport that is high risk, for the gravity of the undertaking doesn't lend itself to too much light-heartedness. But having "fun" is probably defined differently by those climbing at 20,000 feet with limited oxygen and frostbite than by those at sea level in front of a fireplace. For them, laying siege to the mountain is fun.

Not so for the entrepreneurs. Focused as they are on reaching that goal, they are equally as determined to enjoy the endeavor as much as possible. They work hard and they play hard and manage to keep their eye on the ball in both social and professional arenas. They want to have more fun than workaholics. These creative, brave and affable self-starters want to live life to the fullest and are incredibly adept at making that happen. In fact, they often find humor in the idiosyncrasies of human nature and see compromise around them as part of dealing with people.

Despite the many complexities in the nature of her relationships, when a mountain climber decides that a person is special to her, there is no more loyal or attentive companion. These women wrestle with the pulls of their true love—the mission—and with the demands of working through their relationships with people. Interestingly, at fifty, the workaholics we interviewed—now all highly successful professionally—are refocusing their energy more into the people and relationships that matter to them. Making new and maintaining old personal connections are high priorities. For entrepreneurs, people are also more important than ever.

Planned Spontaneity

Jan, a successful executive in a large city, recalls that once when she was in her early thirties she went through a phase when she did nothing but work and rarely did anything with her husband or friends that didn't help in some way with her professional goals. After a time, however, she seemed more stressed than usual and began to make uncharacteristic mistakes. Colleagues and her husband discussed their concerns with her and she reluctantly agreed to try to have "more fun." She called several people she hadn't seen for a while and asked them if they were free to come to her house for a cookout the following weekend. "I have scheduled some unstructured time and would love to see you," she explained antiseptically. She was teased about her choice of words for years to come.

Even in her early fifties, Jan admits that she doesn't "roll with the punches" much. Once, during a peer review session, her colleagues, who genuinely respected her, told her that she was "anal-retentive" and sometimes difficult to work with. Another time, as Jan prepared for a project, her secretary made a big mistake that would take days to repair. Upset, Jan dressed her down. Through tears, her secretary blurted out, "I'm sorry. It's my mistake and I'll fix it. But everything and everyone must be perfect for you or someone pays the price. It will cost me— not you—more time to get it the way you want it. But I know as well as you do that when it's done, you will come out on top— as always. So give me a break here!"

The need to have control is a characteristic of some mountain climbers—especially the workaholics. Constantly aware that a sudden storm can arise at any moment and force them to change course mid-climb, they feel an intense need to control what they can. This includes the more "controllable" aspects of a project—the equipment, the food and to a certain extent, the people who are there to help them.

The entrepreneurs want control also, but they recognize their limitations in terms of managing other people and situations. Their approach is to try to influence circumstances to their advantage, but in such a way that sensitivity for the others involved can somehow be preserved. Rather than control people, they would be much more likely to limit their association with those who don't help them. Or they try to win over those who stand in the way.

Proud to be Humble

Marie looked at the bouquet of flowers. The Provost of her university had sent them to her when she was selected as the first tenured female professor in the business college. She had worked so hard for so long and in the face of obstacles that would have deterred most other climbers. She had made it. While speaking at a party the department held in her honor, she modestly credited her colleagues and the staff with much of the success of the program she had created. Mountain climbers know that they can't get to the top without the help of the other climbers and the guides. But in her heart, she knew that her ability to keep the final destination in sight and mastermind the plan ultimately made the climb happen.

Throughout her life, she had hungered for respect and she felt she had finally earned it. The view from the top was indeed as spectacular as she had imagined.

Marie had always assumed that she would be euphoric when she finally reached her destination. But to her surprise, she had mixed feelings. Why? After years of climbing with one purpose at the center of every day's activities, what would follow? Now she was haunted by the fear that there was only one way to go—down. While there's grim satisfaction from struggling upwards, the descent can be just as dangerous, especially to an ego. Much of the prestige that comes with achievements like scaling the highest peaks is earned because ambitious climbers take the most unforgiving routes. Marie had managed this and was enjoying the admiration of those who couldn't or wouldn't attempt the journey or of other climbers who knew all too well how hard it was to get there. John Krakauer found that, "achieving the summit of a mountain was tangible, immutably concrete and the hazards lent the activity a seriousness of purpose that was sorely missing from the rest of my life." Marie wondered what her purpose would be now.

After climbing the highest peaks in the world, climbers can fall into two categories: those who want to bask in the accomplishment but have no desire to do it again and those who are already planning for the next climb, some perhaps as guides. The women in this group fit into these two possible categories as well. The ones who hope to bask in their accomplishment want a graceful descent from the mountain. They are proud of what they have done but they now plan to spend some time doing some things totally unrelated to what had been their all-consuming goal. No matter how exciting the venture was, Marie knows she doesn't want to repeat it. She plans to retire completely at 55 from the university and spend several years sailing. She doesn't rule out the possibility of occasional consulting but she won't go looking for those opportunities.

On the other hand, Toby wants to retire in four years and

help others up the mountain as a guide. She feels that it will then be time for her to move on, that she will have contributed significantly to her company and made a difference to many people. Her responsibilities over the years have expanded dramatically and she now spends much of her time bringing people together, facilitating productive communication, serving as a liaison to numerous community groups. She wants possibly to do some consulting, continue her responsibilities on community boards and perhaps even open up a catering business. She likes mentoring young women who may be facing the array of obstacles she encountered and wants to do more with them. She also wants to continue her role as a regular motivational speaker for colleges and other groups whose members have found inspiration in her experiences. She knows she'll be busy and her biggest fear is that people will discover that she has a more flexible schedule. "It's hard for me to say 'no' when people need me."

Working Hard to Relax

All of the mountain climbers in our study are certain that no matter what they decide to do with the second phase of their lives, they will be happy and successful. And why not? After all, they had blindly entered the unknown before. They were excited about doing it again. What could be so hard about finding a brand new way to "retire?" They know one thing for sure; they will not do it as others do. After all, according to the famous climber Walt Unsworth, "one great advantage which inexperience confers on the would-be mountaineer is that he is not bogged down by tradition or precedence. To him all things appear simple, and he chooses straightforward solutions to the problems he faces."

These are well-organized, focused women whose approach to life has served them well in so many ways. They are not likely to change a pattern that has made them so happy. More than likely, they will give the post-mountain phase of their lives lots of attention before they actually embark. They speak in specific terms about the many things they are going to do to relax. Their days will include such activities as teaching, writing, traveling, cooking, consulting, reading—probably all in one day! To anyone else, of course, it sounds like a pretty full load. But to them, the next phase of their lives will represent a different kind of mountain—one which allows for side trails on the way up and more leisurely picnics on the top.

Chapter 10

THE DISTANCE RUNNER

"Please help me do this alone."

SHE packed her bags and left. At fifty, the age when her mother had begun to slow down and enjoy her life, Ashley planned to start hers. She had worked hard for thirty years, earning respect from her bosses and colleagues, along with countless promotions, the most recent a prestigious position with a federal agency in Washington. But Ashley began to ask herself, "Is that all there is?" Only half way through life, she wanted something more.

She was becoming impatient with bureaucrats and the incessant demands on her time. Managing numerous volumes of research was no longer satisfying and she began to think about leaving. Such thoughts were not foreign to Ashley. She had been restless before and didn't hesitate to leave personal or professional commitments that she found stifling. She always leaped at opportunities to stretch her horizons. Friends and family who had observed this pattern for years thought she had finally found the perfect job, but she bolted again. They cautioned her against taking such a financial and personal risk at her age. But she was euphoric and ready for the ultimate challenge.

She escaped to her hometown to begin a completely new and unfamiliar business, all her very own. Finally, Ashley had the opportunity to do the things she considered important. Her years studying effective communication now could make a difference. She knew that starting over was hard; no doubt the stakes were high. But she was confident she would be able to succeed. The start-up costs and organizational demands meant she would be operating on a shoestring but she was ready, eager, and prepared.

*　　*　　*

Ashley's approach to life is typical of a distance runner. Consider the pattern. A runner approaches the starting line, ready for the race. It's a test of the quality of the daily training, endured for weeks, months, and years, preparing her for mastering this—her current challenge. She is competing with the other runners, but more significantly, she is competing with herself. She thinks her strategy through very carefully and has defined a particular objective for today. She will aim to run her fastest time ever, improving her personal best by three seconds. Depending on the results, she will then decide on her strategy for the next race. Maybe she'll try to skim three seconds from her time, perhaps more, or maybe she'll skip the next race altogether. She and only she decides what she will do, race by race and practice by practice. She will hear her coach's advice and her teammates' encouragement, but win or lose, she is the ultimate judge of whether or not she is a success.

The casual observer views distance runners as serene and solitary keepers of their own counsel, appearing to retreat into themselves as they glide effortlessly for miles, steady and determined. They feel the most alive when they are running. They set their own pace and chart their own course as they train, dreaming of ways to improve in more effective and unusual ways and always pushing themselves to the max in competition. Despite their image of being in control, they are sometimes impatient with others as they attempt to create a new and original way of "winning." The process can be exhausting but also preserves for them a sense of freedom that is essential for their well being.

They make it look easy. Put on your running shoes and run. But it is not. Perhaps surprisingly, it is often extremely hard on these women. In fact, it is a much more involved process than most might imagine. It requires mental discipline and involves interaction with other solitary runners whose support helps the runner achieve her goals. But such is the nature of the sport.

Distance runners can be either very solitary women on the one hand or very self-sufficient women on the other. Most find themselves somewhere in the middle of these two extremes. The isolated women have chosen to trust their instincts alone, almost always dismissing the suggestions of others. They prefer to be by themselves as often as possible and see days spent reflecting, reading and determining their own path as the most productive. People can get in they way, becoming obstacles on their running trail.

Self-sufficient runners are quite different. Although they value time alone as key to their well being, they also find stimulation in others. They enjoy people and try to make use of their suggestions as they chart their course. They may draw on others' ideas for inspiration but know they will make their own decisions. They rarely depend on anyone for anything, if they can help it, but value social interactions as rewarding and fun.

Independent yet Dependent

Distance runners are fiercely independent. Frank Sinatra was singing for them when he belted out, "I did it my way." They are gentle rebels who follow their instincts both personally and professionally, often having numerous jobs during the course of their lives. While they enjoy talking about their plans and sharing feelings with friends and colleagues, they rarely follow the suggestions of others unless these happen to support a decision that they have already made on their own.

Charlotte changed jobs six times in eight years during her forties when she decided to "follow my heart instead of being stifled by doing what others want or expect me to do." Well-trained with a doctorate in counseling, she is one of those lucky people who is always able somehow to find another good job, or at least "good" by her standards. She lived in Colorado, New Mexico and Hawaii and was everything from a waitress to a corporate trainer. Unfortunately, she suffered severe, almost debilitating back pain. Trusted friends and family urged her to take a job that provided health benefits. But she ignored all of these warnings because "everything will be all right. I can handle it." During one bad episode, the man with whom she was living rushed her to the hospital for emergency care only to discover that doctors would not treat her unless she had insurance. They left the hospital, returning twenty minutes later, married, so that she would be covered by his policy. She made sure that the next job she took had excellent health benefits. But her independence almost cost her her life—at least as she knew it.

Runners must have miles of open space in order to run long distances. They also have to be flexible in of choosing the best trails. This is also true of the women in this type. They need a lot of room to be who they are, both in their work environments and in their relationships. Almost two-thirds of the women interviewed chose to remain single, half of those having never been married at all. Of the married ones, several expressed ambivalence about the institution of marriage even though they clearly love their husbands.

Sara has been married to Jim for twenty-five years and has, at times, felt confined and trapped by the daily responsibilities and the predictable tensions that result from living with a husband and two children. She seriously considered leaving on several occasions and living alone but finally decided that she would stay married—ironically "in order to keep her freedom." She has concluded that she "will have to give up too much" in terms of lifestyle, income and the particulars of maintaining a home if she has to handle everything on her own. There would be no more spur of the moment dinners with friends if there were no one at home to feed the dog. No more extended trips to conferences if no one is able to get bills in the mail or let the repairmen in to fix the washer. It's a compromise for her, but a trade-off that will allow her to continue to do things her way.

Leaning on others for support does not come easily for these women. Ashley tells of an exercise that she participated in during her thirties that was designed to help the participants assess their understanding of teamwork. All of the participants but one were to make a tight circle. The one left out (Ashley, in this case) was to "try to get into the circle any way possible." When Ashley came into the room, she quickly determined that her strategy would be to find the weakest link in the group and force herself into the middle. She took a running start and broke thorough, roughly breaking apart the hands of the two unsuspecting weak links. During the discussion following, the participants told her how surprised they were by this aggressive maneuver, especially since she was usually rather quiet and mild-mannered. One of them finally asked, "Did it ever occur to you just to ask us to let you in?" Ashley describes this incident as the first time that she realized how reluctant she was ever to ask for assistance. "It never occurred to me before then that my first inclination when I need something is always to get it for myself." Interestingly, Sara described playing the same game in a completely different part of the country. When it was her turn to get into the circle, she showed the same independence as Ashley, but in a different way. She simply refused to play. "Fine," she said, "don't let me in." And she walked away.

Ironically, while distance runners inevitably make the

final decisions about their personal or work lives, they rely on others for support to act as sounding boards and outside gauges for their progress. They need the combined energy of teammates during the day-to-day training sessions and even during races. Women in this type say that the support and encouragement of others is a critical element as they plan actions for themselves and take on new challenges both personally and professionally. They experience a true camaraderie with the other runners who are the only ones, they believe, who can truly understand how they think and how critical their doing it alone is to them.

Where does this independence and desire to take the road less traveled come from? Perhaps surprisingly, the women interviewed in this group were reared in traditional homes where there were strong parental influences. In fact, most said their mothers were their role models. Their mothers often were homemakers but had an independent streak. Several said their mothers were negative role models whose lifestyle they wanted to avoid—an "anti-model," as one put it.

For example, Charlotte is the daughter of parents who were hard-working, church-going people with definite ideas about how life should be lived. They were loving but strict parents who expected her to toe the line and lead a life like they had. She lived in one house through all her years of growing up, and the family rarely traveled anywhere other than to visit relatives. When she graduated from high school, she wasn't clear about many things for her life, but one thing she knew for sure—she wanted to go far away. She married a military man and spent the next several years in Germany. She thrives on travel and learning about foreign cultures. Even though she loves her mother, she still dreads visits home where she feels confined, limited and claustrophobic. In her case, her mother's life represents everything she doesn't want.

Always Another Question

Distance runners typically don't accept much at face value. They are not hesitant about asking hard questions about most everything and usually follow up their questions with more questions. They don't see this as putting people on the spot as much as simply gaining some insight or clarification. For example, one of the questions we asked was: "When do you expect to retire?" Most women quickly answered with a simple "At age 60", or "As soon as I have enough money." Not distance runners. They peppered us back with questions. "That depends. What do you mean by retire? Do you mean from my present job? Or from any job I might have in the future? Or do you mean from any organized definition of work? Are you defining retirement as the absence of work altogether? When you say 'you,' do you really mean 'me' or do you really mean 'anyone?' When you say 'expect,' do you mean when do I hope to retire or when do I assume I will retire?"

Distance runners often find that some people are threatened by such questions; they're too analytical. Ashley once asked her supervisor what he thought would be the perfect job for her. He responded that it would have to be in a place where people would not be uncomfortable with her questions. The need to know the truth about situations and be comfortable with them is key to their being true to themselves.

These women often find that they cannot join others in accepting the status quo. Just as marathoners are hard on themselves if they don't perform well, they can be brutally honest about their own shortcomings that created the results. They plan to work harder for the next challenge and vow to better their time. Likewise, these women want to change and improve things wherever they are and they see asking the hard questions as a way to do this. It is not unusual for them to be the ones to say that the emperor is not wearing any clothes. They always call things as they see them, even if it costs them, which it often does. It's a matter of principle and they can do nothing else.

Succeeding on Whose Terms?

Distance runners define success for themselves and resist conforming to other people's definition of it. They usually have a clear vision of their short-range goals but are not wedded to a single, long-range outcome. One referred to it as her "Scarlet O'Hara Syndrome," which lets her remember that "tomorrow is another day." For example, while distance runners always want to run the "best race possible," they may not be sure of exactly what that means. And for the time being, it doesn't matter. They are sure that the immediate objective for the next step of the race is to beat Sally or to better their time from the last race. Likewise, though most people might consider being promoted or gaining a prestigious title to be the mark of success, the distance runner may define it as leaving the company altogether and starting over with something completely new.

Like Ashley and Charlotte, Kathleen doesn't hesitate to rebel against conventional views of what is successful or safe. Even in her twenties, when she had a good, solid job teaching high school English in a small town, she "somehow knew" after two years that it was time to leave. Her principal, friends, boyfriend and parents all encouraged her to stay put and work towards a future in a community that appreciated her work. Yet, she felt keenly that even with the successes she had there, she "had been there long enough and that the unknown was better" if she "was going to have more, know more and experience more."

At the same time, our society tends to define the idea of success for all of us and even distance runners are not totally immune to being influenced by the accepted benchmarks of success. If there were no record books kept detailing the accomplishments of runners, would many choose to buy in to the sport at all? Most athletes play to win and even if they know from the beginning that they can't be the best, they want gauges for comparison. Sara reluctantly admits that she was determined for years to own a two-story house like her sister's. "I needed to have it to prove to myself—and to my sister—that I could have it also." The life distance runner is constantly aware of this dilemma although she still struggles to define success on her own terms.

The brave young Kathleen who left a safe, small environment in her twenties went on to teach in a large city. This was one of the first times that she remembers beginning a life-long pattern of putting herself into difficult situations in order to grow and expand her horizons. "I always do the things I'm most afraid of doing. It's enough satisfaction for me to know that I was able to do them." Over time, she found herself caught up in climbing the proverbial ladder of success as defined by the education establishment. After twelve years in the classroom, she completed her masters' degree and was selected for a series of administrative positions leading to principal. These coveted positions brought money, power, and respect that she found attractive and helpful to her self-esteem. She was successful by almost anyone's standard. Throughout her career, however, she expressed disappointment that her need for societal approval as well as financial security had her "trapped" in a job that kept her from her true calling, that of writer and photographer.

Living Short Term—Planning Long Term

For most of her life, Kathleen has been the poster girl for consumerism. She has spent to the limit on every credit card she has, buying everything that struck her fancy and that she could afford. She followed her instincts and, in many cases, indulged her whims, enjoying each paycheck to the fullest. Short-term gratification was her reward for a hard month's work.

While short-term gratification can be satisfying, distance runners learn that they must pace themselves. Unlike sprinters who pour everything into quick bursts of energy, distance runners learn to begin slowly, spreading their energy evenly so that there is enough left for a "kick" at the end. They also know that one does not become a true distance runner by mastering any one workout. This is accomplished only by sheer determination over the course of time.

At this point, most of the boomer runners have a financial plan of some kind to prepare for the future. However, for most of them, this concern had not been reflected as an important priority—until now. Following their dreams of experiencing each race to the fullest, they have spent what it took to do so, leaving little for savings. Charlotte found, after leaving a secure position as a college professor, that her desire to live in Hawaii drained her resources, forcing her at times to accept any job available. It didn't matter—that's what it took. Even now, when she looks back at that decision, she has no regrets, but reality is setting in and putting something aside for the long term is a new but essential priority.

At the same time, distance runners see the sport as a lifelong activity, a lifestyle. They participate in the competitive aspects of the sport when young but alter the purpose for fitness and enjoyment as they get older. Likewise, women in this group do the same thing. Ashley's rise to the highest levels of the governmental bureaucracy is a classic example of her winning career race after career race. She gained valuable knowledge and saved some money. At fifty, she could take all that she had learned and modify the pace of some of the same activities, organizing them into a more manageable and flexible arrangement. Rather than working in a high pressure, 9 to 5 situation, she could continue to contribute in the field as a self-employed consultant but in a way that will be part of the long-term lifestyle that she wants to enjoy for years to come.

Distance runners know about the Greek marathoner Phidippides who ran the "perfect race" and died at the end of it because he gave it everything he had. They respect Phidippides' accomplishment, not just because he was swift, but also because he carried out his plan for the race. Like him, they simply want to run THEIR race. Kathleen said emphatically, "If it's someone else's race, then I don't want to run it at all." Every runner knows that life is a process of taking each step as it comes and that the overall pattern of her life will unfold over time.

Being driven by the short term as they plan for the long term is a phenomenon that plays out in all aspects of the runners' lives. Sara struggles every day with the challenges of rearing an adopted teen-age daughter who's difficult and troubled. She has endured threats, tantrums, and even physical assaults by this girl. She has sat through countless sessions with psychologists in order to help and understand this child who came into the world with many problems. Sara knows what she wants—a healthy, self-sufficient young lady. This goal drives every decision she makes every day. Even though obstacles clutter the running trail, she patiently stays the course.

Finding Inner Peace

Almost all of the boomer runners say that their biggest source of inspiration is reading. They are reflective individuals who enjoy spending hours with books. While recharging their batteries, they need time just to "be" and to think. Afterwards, they feel renewed and energized. At the same time, they do like to talk with others about what they are reading. Despite limited time, more than half join book clubs. One quality they value most in their friendships is discussing and sharing ideas openly. "Friends," said one, "are the light in the dark of life."

Runners described themselves as "spiritual" and strongly believe that spirituality is a personal matter. However, they find comfort and stimulation through contacts with others who view life as they do. Like most of the others, Sara describes herself as more centered at fifty than she has ever been before, feeling more at peace with herself. She says that she is gradually coming to a better understanding of the world and her role in it. These women are also more focused in their intent to develop habits and routines for spiritual study and contemplation. For some, this means more involvement in church and Bible study, for others it includes meditation and yoga. All are seeking an inner peace, or as one woman put it, "growing into a more authentic self."

Confident but Need Validation

Distance runners are confident. After years of training, they develop a strong sense of pride. They know what their bodies can do because they test them every day, pushing them to the limit. Always intuitive, they trust themselves and see themselves as the ultimate authority over their destiny. Kathleen remembers traveling alone in Europe after she graduated from college and being determined to read the train schedule herself without asking for assistance. It may have taken her more time, but she was finally able to decipher it on her own.

Yes, they are definitely sure of themselves in most respects. But they admit that they are often more productive when they work with or even follow the advice of their coaches. Women runners say that their coaches and certain teammates actually serve as role models as they progress through the various stages of their training. They would rather do almost anything than to ask for direct advice. But they will watch those they admire and make note of practices they find valuable. Marsha taught herself to be a photographer. When she landed a part-time job as a "stringer" for the Associated Press, she was keenly aware that she was working with others who were better trained and more highly skilled than she. On her first assignment, she wasn't at all sure of the way she was expected to go about doing things. Rather than ask anyone, she watched the veterans carefully, priding herself on the fact that, not only did no one know she was new, but that she was at least as competent as anyone else.

It is also true that in some cases, runners will choose not to tackle a challenge unless they have direct and specific encouragement. For example, Violet was asked to write a book about areas in her profession for which she had become highly respected. She knew she was a good writer and she felt passionately about her topic. Without the confidence expressed by the publisher and her colleagues, however, she admits that she would never have considered doing it at all.

Pain is Temporary: Pride is Forever

Ann decided in her thirties that she needed more money to buy a house. This meant taking on another job—one that would not interfere with her full-time job as teacher. So she took on a second job—a paper route, getting up at 3:30 am each morning and walking a three-mile route, mostly uphill. It was grueling, but the day she moved into her own home, she knew it was worth the effort.

Like Ann, distance runners accept discomfort as part of the process of winning. They learn to experience and accept the predictable muscle pain, labored breathing, side stitches and overall fatigue in their bodies as they run for miles at a time. Sometimes they can overcome the hurts. Sometimes they can't and must drop out of the race or workout altogether in order to heal or regroup. However, this is always a last resort. The disappointment they feel when they do this is the biggest part of the pain. They are not only disappointed in themselves, but fear that they have somehow not met the expectations of others. Still, there is no let-up and the tempo for the most part is always moderate and steady. They accept the discomfort as temporary and part of the sport.

Meeting a challenge becomes familiar for these women. They know that sacrifice is part of reaching a goal. When Ashley left her responsible position with a federal agency and moved to a small city, she carried out her plan of settling down. After five years, she decided to limit her consulting business and accept a less prestigious job that was mundane but useful. Soon, however, an unexpected opportunity arose. A large organization in another part of the country offered her an excellent position for which she was well qualified. This meant starting over—again. But it also meant new possibilities for achievement, growth, and satisfaction. With little hesitation, she decided to move and endure the hassles of another beginning, another leg of the race.

Because they understand the need for pacing over time, distance runners roll with the punches. And they have become good at it. They strive daily for balance in all aspects of their lives as they face each challenge. Almost all of these women say that one of the things they are most proud of is the way they have tried to balance their responsibilities in life. Even looking back, they would change very little about how they have managed things. They know they must keep their priorities straight and accept each day as another opportunity to better their performance from the day before. The key is to keep training, to stay the course, and to prepare for unexpected turns on the trail. But the most important thing is to enjoy the run.

PART III

WINNING THE GAME

Chapter 11

BABY BOOM WOMEN AND RETIREMENT

"Is there life after work?" mused a group of baby boom women.

"February 2005 at 4:00pm. That's it. I'm through. (Baseball Player)

"I'm not even going to think about it until my stock portfolio at least doubles." (Runner)

"I don't worry about that so much, but I want to be sure that I'm doing something I care about doing." (Sailor)

"Yeah. Besides baby-sitting my husband!" (Cheerleader)

"I'm happy just like I am. I get as much time off as I want already. I don't need to retire." (Lap Swimmer)

Retirement is a word most often associated with someone's decision to quit work—usually a man's decision. When a man says he is going to retire, we have visions of his being out on the golf course, reading a book, or gathering at the local hangout to have coffee. It is clearly connected in our minds with a shift in the way he spends his time, in the roles he will play, and the money he will earn. After heeding the call of the alarm clock for so many years, he is awarded the luxury of setting his own schedule, walking to the beat of his own drum, and enjoying the fruits of his many years of labor.

What about women? Baby boom women will be the first generation of professional women to approach retirement age having spent a significant part of their lives working full-time. Most have careers that span anywhere from 20-30 years. They have earned a living wage, paid social security taxes, invested in 401 (K)s, and spent 8-10 hours a day (often more) for these many years on the job. Do they deserve to retire? Of course. Will they retire in a similar manner as men? Not likely.

One obvious reason is that women do not have a wife, nor do they want one. The roles of wife and mother are important to them. They like managing the household, caring for family members, and volunteering in the community. These women have worked in their careers and *then* worked at home. Therefore, retiring from a job means leaving behind only a part of their total "work" life. Many of the jobs they have held while they also worked outside the home will continue without interruption. What is the likelihood of a woman retiring from that position as "CEO of the household?" Will she hire a cook, a housekeeper, a gardener, and a chauffeur so that she can live the life of leisure? Probably not.

Studies of women and retirement suggest that women are not prepared for this step. The average life expectancy of baby boom women is 84. The average age of widowhood in the United States is 56. Over 58% of baby boom women have less than $10,000 saved in a pension plan of some type. These statistics, from a study done by the National Center for Women and Retirement Institute, are sobering. Baby boom women are going to live almost a third of their lives after the usual age of retirement. More than likely, they are going to spend a significant part of that time alone. Most do not have enough money to support the lifestyles they have established during their working years. Not a pretty picture.

"A woman's personality matters far more than her income, age, or marital status when it comes to making financial decisions," Dr. Christopher L. Hayes concludes from a national study of 4200 baby boom men and women. Assertiveness, openness to change, and an optimistic outlook make for smart financial decisions. Dr. Hayes found women were actually more concerned about career decisions than they were about retirement. As men neared retirement, however, they were far more concerned about their marriages and personal relationships. Fifty-one percent of baby boom men planned to retire at 65. Only 45% of the women wanted to then, with more women than men planning never to retire. Men and women perceive the term differently. Women see retirement as new opportunities; men see it as leisure time. Hayes also found that more women were interested in pursuing important social causes in retirement than men.

We found the same phenomenon among our boomers. The women we interviewed have given very little thought to exactly how or when they will retire. As articulate as they are about themselves and every aspect of their lives, they have virtually nothing to say about the retirement phase of their lives. The very idea is alien to many of them. If circumstances force them to, then of course, they have no choice. Such circumstances might include failing health, being needed by a family member, or changes in the workplace that force them out. They try to control what they can, however, attempting to ward off health problems by exercising regularly and eating properly.

By far the most frequent reasons given for retiring were health problems. There is a vague recognition that they are not immune to them, but one senses that these women, who have for so long done everything they wanted to, don't expect to give anything up unless it's on their terms. The pace of their professional lives in many cases has speeded up—not slowed down—as they have reached their fifth decade. They seem to be in denial regarding their own mortality. They eat, drink, and work as if there is no tomorrow, or as if every tomorrow is promised to them just as today!

When asked what they expect their retirement to be like, the most common response was "lots of travel." But how much can one travel? What will they do once they get back from these elusive trips? To travel and avoid sickness seems to be the bulk of their current retirement plan.

Financial concerns are also important considerations of the women we interviewed. After all, how does one afford all of this travel? Most say that they have savings accounts and are beginning to talk to financial managers. Some are investing in stock portfolios as security. They know that money can make a tremendous difference in the quality of their lives later—as it does now. Even though they are making some headway in terms of shoring up their financial assets, many of the women are still not sure exactly how much will be required or how long these resources will last.

Some are concerned about dimensions of their retirement life that they have virtually ignored for many years. They have spent so much time caring for their families and doing their jobs that they have few outside interests to fill the vacuum when they leave their careers. For those whose support system has been largely made up of colleagues from work, there are real fears of loneliness and isolation. "You can't take these relationships and day-to-day contacts home like you can the gold watch after the good-bye party," said one.

The Retirement Person "Fit"

Just as the work setting "fits" for one person and not another, so too the retirement plan for one boomer is not likely to "fit" the needs of all boomers. The cheerleader is not likely to define or envision retirement in the same way as the runner. To look at the differences is to be reminded that all baby boom women are not alike.

Retirement represents the last leg of another race for the runner. As such, it is viewed in the same way as the current race. The runner herself insists on deciding what she will do with her retirement. She may ask many questions, seek out experts, look to models, but in the end, she will "do it her way." The runner is not fearful of retirement. She is aware that it takes money and is beginning to look for opportunities for saving it. She is clear that no one will dictate the terms of her retirement, telling her how to spend either her days or her money. "Say no!" insisted one runner. She wasn't about to jump into everything she might be asked to do. She plans to guard her time and commit only to projects she values. The runner is more definite about what she is *not* going to do than what she is going to do.

The mountain climber will define retirement as another peak to be mastered, or possibly as the other side of a mountain already climbed. If she sees it as another mountain, she is likely to identify other challenges she can embrace, such as a second career. She may even pursue the career she has secretly imagined through the years as an escape. After a successful twenty-five years in real estate, one boomer decided to become an artist full time. She decorated her studio and began selling her work in galleries.

The climber's greatest fear is a loss of status. What is a mountain climber with no mountain? Just a person with a rope. The mountain climber may mentor other women with similar interests and bask in the success of those she leads. She may be the one who joins a social club and attempts to treat it like a job, alienating the rest of the members who are there primarily to have a good time. Harriet was a successful educational consultant. She gave up her job and moved to another part of the country where her reputation was unknown. Lonely, she joined a local friendship building organization, quickly rising to the role of vice-president. Unfortunately, she forgot that it was a voluntary group and began to dictate regulations, chastising those who did not follow her directives. Harriet made no friends. In fact, she almost destroyed the organization with her authoritarian approach. She is a climber who forgot to be sure that there was indeed a mountain to be climbed before she climbed all over the people around her.

The martial artist's greatest fear of retirement is a loss of power to champion her causes. Interestingly, when asked whether they'd like to dabble in politics, most of the women we interviewed quickly dismissed the idea. But they want to engage in community service. "I don't see them as anything alike," said one boomer. These women are not going to go gently into that good night. They will find ways to contribute to the lives of those around them. The advocates will be welcome additions to boards and service agencies, volunteer groups and political committees. The warriors, armed with their swords, may find that their manner is too cutting. What they were able to pull off in the work place may not happen in the "volunteer place." One boomer recognizes that her style may not translate as well away from work. "I know that I am not patient with people who don't have the same political views that I do," she says. "But if we aren't all on the same page, how will we get anything accomplished? This could be a problem for me." Some of the warriors say they are considering more solitary routes, such as writing. These women are sure that whatever their retirement holds, they refuse to depend on anyone. So they want to have the income and health to remain independent.

The sailors' plans revolve around fulfillment and flexibility. They are more balanced in their preparation for retirement, looking at income, social support, and outside interests. They fear most a loss of meaning in what they do daily, often using words such as "boring" to suggest a life with no important challenges. The needs of other family members have a major influence on their decisions to retire.

Baseball players were the most definite about their retirement plans of all the groups we interviewed. They have successfully compartmentalized their work life and their home life and pride themselves on feeling successful in both places. Since they have a full life away from work, they don't face this step with the same degree of concern that many of the other groups did. Most had plans to keep working until full retirement benefits were available and the needs of their family were met. "I'm leaving as soon as my last child graduates from college," said one. They look forward to not having to deal with the daily grind of work. One boomer said, "I want to fill my days doing just what I want to do. It will be a pleasure not to have to plan my activities around the needs of the hospital." Many of the women say that they want to spend more time volunteering—"something I know will give me a feeling of usefulness," as one put it, "but one that lets me determine where, when and how often I do it." The fact that work has not consumed their entire life helps them enter the next decades more comfortably.

The lap swimmers anticipate working for as long as they can. The type of work they do as well as their approach to doing it allows them to make more leisurely decisions about retirement. Interestingly, when asked what they looked forward to the most about retirement, many of them said travel. Perhaps the confines of the pool make them eager to break out of their world and see what's there. Financial considerations are also an important part of their decisions. For those who are lap swimming in a pool like teaching, nursing or working in a bureaucracy, their salaries may be mediocre at best.

The cheerleaders define retirement in terms of their husband's decision to stop work. As one boomer said, "Retirement? I'm already retired." For the most part, they have made no preparation from a financial standpoint, trusting their spouse to ensure their security. "I have no fears because, in truth, nothing will change—except for the fact that Harry will be home all the time," says one. Then reconsidering, "Wait a minute. A lot may change!" She'll likely continue to cheer him on—even if it's only on the golf course. Since their lives have largely been centered on his career, his needs become more ambiguous, as do hers. Family demands continue to be the primary focus of the cheerleader's days. She looks forward to helping with grandchildren, aging parents, troubled friends and will do so with pleasure.

Reshaping the Dream

Louise is a 91-year-old businesswoman who regularly mentors baby boom women. She lives alone, drives her own car, attends church every Sunday, and has as busy a social life as any of her young neighbors. She lives life to the fullest. She spent over 30 years in the book business, managing three bookstores. Louise was happily married, raised her three children, and has been active in her church and community all her life. She was a mountain climber before her time, a true trailblazer. She has earned the right to speak her mind, and speak it she does. She's a good model for our generation.

"When I retired, I packed my car up, backed out of the driveway, and never looked back," Louise recalls. "Each phase of life has its own plateaus with hills and valleys on either side. When its time to move on, then do it—with no regrets." Louise sits erect, her mind sharp and decisive. She has no hesitation when asked questions about the idea of retirement, hers or that of these young boomer women.

Louise shares a list she made of twenty-five things she is thankful for. One, "memories," jumps out. "I'm thankful for my memories. I can go back and visit the past anytime I wish. But I have to live in the present." She is on a crusade to stop women from giving up at 50. Her formula for happiness is based on faith, family, and friendship. "Paying attention to all three will always prepare you for what's next."

Our baby boom women should do just that. Many already are. Hungrier for spiritual growth, they are joining Bible study groups, meditating and exploring a variety of personal journeys. These women who had for so long run the race, stayed the course, jumped the hurdles, fought the good fight, are now looking within themselves to explore the meaning in their lives.

Retirement is a "crisis." The Chinese symbol for crisis is twofold: danger and opportunity. For baby boomers, it will surely be both. In ancient times, menopausal women were viewed as sources of wisdom. Just like Louise, the boomer women will have to provide guidance and direction to others. A nationally known spokeswoman for women's issues, Joan Borysenko, points out that middle-aged women go through another stage in their lives—being a guardian. "The guardian possesses a visionary wisdom needed to protect our fragile circle of life," Borysenko writes. Our boomers will be those guardians and have much to teach. The cheerleader will protect her family, making sure that all are nurtured and loved. The mountain climber will blaze trails for others to follow to reach the top. The sailor will teach balance between home and work. The baseball player will share the joy of winning as a team. The runner will nurture the idea that solitude is a source of strength and power. The martial artist will demonstrate that some things are worth fighting for. The lap swimmer will model the elegance of staying the course, no matter how long.

Boomer women have had five decades to hone their wisdom. They have known sorrows and joys, births and deaths, wins and losses. The struggle to define what retirement is for them will no doubt be another source of angst for some. But based on their past, they will surely approach each new day with gusto.

Chapter 12

CONCLUSIONS

"What is one scoop of ice cream? A very good start!"

JULIE stops for ice cream every afternoon after work. She limits herself to one scoop of her favorite flavor. But today is different. Today she savors every bite and decides to treat herself to another scoop. Why not? But now, for the difficult part. What flavor? What size? What topping? Should she take it home for later?

As the boomers enter "Phase II," the second part of their adult lives, they are much like Julie. They have savored every part of their first scoop—the combination of home and work life. Satisfied with the past, they look ahead to the future with optimism. They haven't figured out exactly what it will look like, but they know they want it to be just as rich as "Phase I."

These are women who have respected and tried to preserve the traditional approaches that their mothers lived. This means putting the family first, nurturing those they care for, and tending to the home fires. But they also wanted to add an important dimension to their lives, that of career, a dimension that had been denied to their mothers in many ways. Straddling the old traditional values and their new roles as professionals has proved to be a challenging yet a rewarding experience for baby boom women. In the professional arena, they played by the rules of the game without hesitation, knowing this would be the way to "win." But they didn't stop there. They wanted to change the rules, not only for themselves, but also for future generations of women. They were sure they had a better way of doing things and deliberately tried to find ways to make changes occur. They did what they had to do to get their ticket punched—and then compete.

For the most part, these middle-class boomer women are an extremely satisfied group—satisfied with the way they balanced their lives, satisfied with their families, and satisfied with their professional achievements. They are optimistic about their futures and their abilities to handle whatever comes their way. At this point, they feel a sense of control over their circumstances and over how they will manage the years to come.

Of all the groups, the most satisfied were, by far, the sailors. These are the consummate straddlers between conventional and unconventional approaches. They apparently have achieved their overall goal of "having it all," which for them meant an equal emphasis on the traditional (home and family) and the non-traditional (career). Clearly, most wanted to be mothers (embracing biology) but only as part of their destiny. Combining roles allowed them to have security and strike out on new paths, to be conventional and to pioneer. They joined continuity with change.

Almost without exception, boomers claim that family is and always has been their first priority. They have turned down promotions, refused to move, quit jobs, and sacrificed personal ambition to be wives and mothers. We also know that they have achieved this great measure of satisfaction without the assistance of clear role models. In fact, most of those we interviewed said they had none. While they admired many women, they couldn't identify role models who exemplified what they believed to be women worthy of emulation.

These women are also entering Phase II with a renewed sense of the value of the friendships that they have enjoyed over the years. Having women friends has contributed to the satisfaction they have experienced during their lives. Without exception, every boomer we interviewed emphasized a need to keep old friends and make new ones.

The Legacy of Contradictions

Baby boom women inherited a legacy of tradition based on clear messages from society. With the encouragement of their mothers, they created a new reality fraught with contradictions. These contradictions have made them who they are—complex and interesting. Whether or not they intended to, they have passed these contradictions on to their daughters along with the family china.

While boomers are usually sure about the messages they want to give their daughters, they are much less sure about what messages the daughters actually received. For example, one boomer, Lena, was surprised to find a big discrepancy between the ways she and her daughter, Elise, describe work. As she was preparing to graduate from college, Elise once said, "Mom, your generation had it easy. You had a choice of whether or not to work. I've known from day one that I had better get a good job and plan to take care of myself." Lena was pleased that Elise had plans to be self-sufficient but was surprised in several ways at this statement. Lena doesn't recall telling Elise that she must be totally self-sufficient. In fact, her daughter had been reared with more financial security than Lena or her husband had ever dreamed of providing. Their family had clearly enjoyed a privileged lifestyle. Her family could support her financially if needed no matter what career she pursued. Obviously, Lena had passed on her own middle-class work ethic to her children, which pleased her. Lena was also surprised that Elise thought her mother had a choice about work, especially since Elise had heard stories all her life about how

Lena had been working since she was twelve. "We have what we have because we have worked every day of our lives," says Lena. "Why is it that she hasn't made that connection?"

Another daughter, Mindy, told her boomer mother, Etta, how lucky Etta had been to have gone to graduate school in the late sixties. "As a female in those days, you had special status as a minority applicant," says Mindy. "That's not true today. I'm no different from anybody else. It's going to be a lot harder for me to get in." Mindy may be right. What an irony! The hard work of the baby boomers through the years to level the playing field has actually hurt some of our children's chances for getting a leg up.

We have tried hard to become the role models we wished we had. While we want to be valued and respected for the paths we have chosen, we now encourage our daughters to look to themselves for answers. We don't want them limited by any one perspective as they define their identities at home and at work.

Finally, one of the biggest contradictions of all concerns choices. We have always pushed for as many choices in as many areas of life as possible. And we got them. We have come to expect choices—salad bars with twenty items, malls that cover acres, six shades of mauve from which to select paint for our bedrooms, and several payment plans so that we can have what we want and when we want it. Faced with the countless options, it's no surprise that there is a growing movement for a return to simplicity. We are sometimes overwhelmed by the choices— even the trivial choices we make every day. One boomer said, "I can't stand to shop for anything anymore. There is so much to see and to pick from that it exhausts me. Too much!!"

There is no longer any professional door closed to our daughters. In fact, there are now more women in college than men. This creates a new dilemma for the twenty-somethings— which career to choose. One boomer's daughter expressed her frustration when she called home from college for advice: "How can I decide on one major when there are so many great departments to pick from? I want to go to med school but teaching might be good, too. Of course, I'd have a good future if I went into some area of technology. I'll just wait and maybe it will come to me later. By the way, I have a chance to go abroad next semester. Should I pick England, Italy or Germany?" The choices we made possible for them won't stop there. They can choose to have children or not—with a husband or not. They can buy a car or lease a car. They can live with a roommate or by themselves. Who would ever have thought that the task of making a decision in the midst of so many choices could also be so frustrating for many.

The New Reality: Life with a Serious Sense of Humor

Baby boom women have never been more aware than they are now that life's circumstances can change in a flash. The death of a spouse, the development of a disease, the loss of a child are all realities that seem almost a daily consideration. They are looking for ways to prepare for such possibilities. Many are seeking more meaning in what they do. They are looking for spiritual direction to sustain them through dark times.

Life is serious, but maintaining a "joie de vivre" is critical. Many of the women say that having a sense of humor has been critical to their maintaining equilibrium in the face of turmoil. The ability to laugh at themselves and, to the extent possible, their problems, is essential to a healthy outlook. We found that, in many cases, those who seemed to have confronted the most serious issues were, in fact, often the best able to find humor in daily situations that help them cope more effectively. They also gravitate towards others who can make them laugh.

The seven types of baby boom women we identified are clearly different from each other. Too long have women been divided by their differences. At this point in our lives, we can only be strengthened and enriched by accepting those same differences and learning from each other. We hope the cheerleader who places high priority on home and family will appreciate the relentless task-orientation of the mountain climber. Likewise, the distance runner who values independence can also appreciate the baseball player's need to be on a team.

*   *   *

We're different. We're not the women our mothers were or even the women we thought we'd be. For the most part, we have done things our way and at fifty we are confident that we have only begun to enter Phase II—which has the potential to be the most rewarding, glorious and relaxing time of our lives. It's time to enjoy what we have worked so hard to have. Many feel that everything up to now has been some sort of "preparation"—and we are prepared. Even now, we believe we have so much to do and time to do it. We are intellectually aware of our mortality but we won't let this detail influence our planning too much. After all, we are the same people who aimed to be the super women of the 70's. Like Julie in the ice cream shop, we expect that second scoop to be just as satisfying, just as flavorful as the first. Boomer women are in the autumn of their lives. As one expressed it so well, "Autumn is truly the most beautiful season of the year."